Praise for

Doing Small Things with Great Love

"We all want to do something good in the world. We should also want to do it well. Sharon's insightful new book provides a road map to help all of us make sure our acts of service are as impactful as they can be. I trust her advice because she has initiated, worked in, and overseen some of the most effective local, national, and global programs I have seen."

—**MICHAEL J. NYENHUIS,** president and CEO
of UNICEF USA

"The book provides thoughtful insights from a true humanitarian leader on how we can all make an impact in our communities and the world. What Sharon shares in these pages and the 12 Principles of Service is a gift for all of us!"

—**MATT BERTRAM,** humanitarian service leader

"This invaluable guide to individual change-making comes from an extraordinary humanitarian who has enabled thousands of people to make a difference. Sharon's framework for answering the question "How can I help?" outlines practical, clear steps for turning love and compassion into action and impact. There has never been a more important moment for mobilizing the power of individuals to drive change, and this book is the perfect place to start."

—**MICHELLE NUNN,** CEO of CARE International

"Whether you are just at the beginning stage of figuring out how to best help others or consider yourself very knowledgeable in serving others, Sharon takes all of us on her journey of storytelling in a meaningful way that no one else can. Sharon has given the world an amazing gift by sharing key principles from her lifelong commitment to humanity and reminds us all that no effort to help our fellow human being is too small."

> —**BARRON SEGAR,** president and CEO of World Food Program USA

"This is a powerful book. It overflows with lessons born of Sharon's deep understanding, broad experience, and rock-solid commitment to the welfare of others. She makes it abundantly clear that the challenge to 'make a difference in the world' is essentially a call to improve our own world, the one in which each of us lives and labors every day. That's where everyone can have an impact and where the miracles take place. We just need to start."

> —**COMMISSIONER KENNETH HODDER,** national commander (ret.) The Salvation Army USA

"Given the turmoil the world is currently facing, the work of everyday humanitarians is more important than ever."

> —**JOHN HEWKO,** general secretary, International Rotary

"A lovely, important, and moving book filled with wisdom and grace. In a time when it seems suddenly fashionable for people to be cruel to strangers, this little gem of a book is timely and sorely needed."

> —**LARRY KEELEY,** innovation scientist and founder of Keeley Innovations LLC

"Sharon Eubank's focus on love linked to action permeates this delightful and inspiring book. The kindness and generosity the book documents rekindle a hope in people's fundamental goodness. And I won't forget one piece of advice: 'Don't let stress ruin the fun.'"

—**KATHERINE MARSHALL,** senior fellow, Berkley Center for Religion, Peace, and World Affairs, Georgetown University; executive director, World Faiths Development Dialogue

"What an incredible and meaningful book! It is so impressive that Sharon not only gives advice about what one can do but also about what one shouldn't do. The emphasis on listening, trust, and relationships is just great for people to read and learn. I also liked how she highlighted the importance of looking at the needs where you live and that one doesn't always have to go to another country to find out how they can help in so many ways. This book is very hard to put down because of the many stories she tells about other people and how they have been able to do small things with great love!"

—**PAMELA ATKINSON,** special adviser to Utah governor

DOING
SMALL THINGS
WITH
GREAT
LOVE

DOING
SMALL THINGS
WITH
GREAT
LOVE

**How Everyday Humanitarians
Are Changing the World**

SHARON EUBANK

**SHADOW
MOUNTAIN
PUBLISHING**

Earthrise image on page 216 by NASA/Johnson Space Center, public domain, https://www.nasa.gov/history/afj/ap08fj/16day4_orbit4.html, rotated. All other interior photos courtesy of the author.

Visit us at shadowmountain.com

Library of Congress Cataloging-in-Publication Data

(CIP data on file)

ISBN 978-1-63993-428-7

Printed in Canada
PubLitho

10 9 8 7 6 5 4 3 2 1

*This book is dedicated to all the sparkling souls
in the world who are relentless for good.*

Contents

Introduction ix

1. The Basics 1

2. You Are Most Powerful Where You Live 23

3. Trusted Networks 43

4. Asking the Right Questions 67

5. Protecting Dignity 95

6. Attacking Root Causes and Nurturing
   Long-Term Solutions 113

7. Volunteerism—The Social Movement 137

8. It's Meant to Be Fun 155

9. Some Final Lessons on What Can and
   Cannot Be Done 177

10. The Work Is Now Yours 195

Reflections 205

Notes 209

Introduction

One day in 1992, I stopped in to visit my parents and found my mom knitting pairs of bright-red slippers to be included in a massive humanitarian airlift aiding besieged Sarajevo. The nightly news was filled with grim stories of the starvation and violence gripping Bosnia and Herzegovina in its ethnic war. I watched my mother casting off stitches and remember thinking to myself, *What good are knitted slippers in the face of all that carnage? Is this the best we can do? Pass out slippers to new widows in a bullet-riddled yard?* I felt dismayed by such paltry efforts when there were so many other palpable needs.

At the time, I didn't see the role those slippers and the questions I was mentally asking about them would play in my future career because I didn't plan to be a humanitarian. I was an English teacher and imagined I would assign essay topics and grade poorly constructed grammar for a long career. But the truth was, those questions were already taking root deep in my psyche. I simply wasn't mature enough yet to answer them. I needed to learn some critical lessons along the way before I could understand the impact of knitted slippers and what they truly stood for.

My first job after university was teaching English language and conversation to Honda employees in Japan who were being transferred to Ohio. These families were on a crash course and were highly motivated to learn practical vocabulary. They asked me to teach them the words for *daikon* and *nori* and all the other foods they hoped to effortlessly buy in Ohio grocery stores. I didn't have the heart to tell them that finding Japanese white radish and sheets of red algae seaweed in Marysville, Ohio, in the late '80s was going to be tricky.

My students were incredibly generous. They coordinated their days off with mine so they could give me the VIP backstage tour of the Honda manufacturing plant. In the hot Japanese summer, they took me to shrines up in the mountains, where it was cool, where I walked under the red torii arch and rang the bell to greet the Shinto gods. They showed me how to observe the proper etiquette in public baths (scrub before you soak!). Once, I walked into the fields behind my apartment and learned how to harvest rice and pile it in little stacks to dry.

My Japanese students taught me things I didn't know I needed to know. When I asked a certain fifth grader in a class of girls what her favorite color was, I was bemused to see a quick council form so the class could agree on the group's favorite color. They would not want to put forward one person's preference without consulting the group. This was a brand-new concept for a woman steeped in the individual, American tradition.

I tried to get my adult conversation students to read a newspaper article and chat with me about the legacy of World War II and how it affected Japanese-American relations now. A kindly woman with evenly trimmed hair and two rowdy teenagers at home finally told me: "It is not polite for me to discuss this topic with you. Please choose another." I thought I was pushing boundaries in an interesting way. She found it impossibly rude. Another lesson for me. I am certain I gained more from my Japanese experience than any of my students ever did.

My next job was working as a staff assistant in the US Senate. The senator I worked for had a leadership office just off the rotunda in the US Capitol. It was the early '90s and First Lady Barbara Bush set the fashion. I wore double-breasted suit jackets with pleated skirts and chunky earrings with plenty of pearls. I was paid a shockingly low salary for the number of hours I worked, but part of the experience was being on the edge of history. I clapped in the audience as Benazir Bhutto addressed a joint session of Congress. I made up a section of the greeting party when Margaret Thatcher sailed into the Capitol on so much charisma that her husband, Dennis, was barely in focus. Robert Redford said he would love some salad and sat at my desk to eat it while waiting for his appointment to start. These were tiny brushes with the movers and shakers of the day, but I had a front-row seat.

However, Washington, DC, was more than brushes with celebrities and politicians. Saddam Hussein invaded Kuwait, and the First Gulf War was broadcast in real time on television. Anita Hill testified before the Senate Judiciary Committee as they voted on a new Supreme Court justice. Major legislation was crafted. Back-office deals were negotiated. Glorious, sordid, heartbreaking, hopeful things all folded together. One of the great lessons I took away was that few experiences are black-and-white. Issues always have multiple sides. Self-righteous anger feels emotionally satisfying, but building bridges of understanding and compromise—plank by plank—across a partisan divide lasts a lot longer if you're trying to do something meaningful.

When the senator I worked for retired, a friend and I determined to pool our savings and open an educational toy store in her hometown. There's nothing more fun than owning a toy store—I still think so—but we didn't start out with enough cash. We intuited quickly that knowing our customers by name and supplying a personal touch were going to be the makings of our under-capitalized business. We jumped in with both feet. After seven years of running a retail establishment through some rough economic waters, two lessons emerged for me: 1) Money is important, but there are other ways to solve problems that should not be discounted. 2) Don't let stress ruin the fun.

It was while I owned the toy store that I read a magazine article referencing a woman caught in Sarajevo during Yugoslavia's civil war. With the city utilities smashed by bombs, she described living in the filthy, dangerous, frigid city and then explained the small pleasure she felt when receiving a pair of new socks. Even more than warmth, she said those socks were a testament that she was human, worthy, and cared about by someone else after she had lost all her family. I thought back to my mother knitting slippers and realized for the first time that what makes assistance valuable isn't the size or the cost but rather that the right thing is delivered at the right time. Ending the war and repairing the city and society were what was ultimately needed, but that wasn't going to happen on that particular day. For that woman on that day, a new pair of socks made a difference. And the fact that they came from another person who was thinking compassionately about her in her situation was an important part of the gift. There is value in doing small things with love.

My friend and I eventually sold the store, and I accepted a job in the humanitarian offices of The Church of Jesus Christ of Latter-day Saints. I didn't have a proper development background, so I engaged in a cycle of different positions to learn the business. I first negotiated ocean containers stuck in customs, learning the ways to sidestep corruption and develop relationships to clear the freight. Next, I worked with entrepreneurs learning the skills to operate their new businesses. I knew from my own business experience the exhilaration of creating something new and the many pitfalls that can derail it. From there, I learned about the dangerous lack of access in most societies for people with disabilities. I spent years working with wheelchair manufacturers on the endless tradeoffs among adjustability, durability, weight, and affordability.

For nine years, I was the regional manager of humanitarian operations in the Middle East during the Syrian war and the rise and fall of ISIS. I witnessed firsthand the intense desperation people feel as they are forced to leave their homes, cross a border, and take on the label of *refugee.*

Now, the most common conversation I have with people is: "I want to do what you are doing. I have a passion for humanitarian work. I feel drawn to helping other people as my mission. What can I do? How can I help?" The second most common conversation I have is: "I feel too small, too isolated to believe my tiny, local efforts matter at all." I have become sensitized to the pent-up desire so many feel to give of themselves and help others with something useful and honorable, and I also have a sense of the fear or self-criticism many have that what they offer will never be enough to make a difference.

Throughout my own somewhat irregular vocational path, I realized I was asking myself similar questions. What can I do? What seemed like unrelated professional jobs were really variations on a single theme: How can I help? Can I as an individual make a real difference, or is it up to governments, organizations, and foundations to do the real work? Do small acts of compassion and connection have power to change situations for the better? If the answer is yes, what's the right way to go about doing it?

I began to think seriously about the underlying principles and assumptions that inform how we treat and help each other. What reliably works? What inadvertently makes things worse? Why isn't it as intuitive as we first believe? How can we translate from the research theory to the practical? What do we learn from our failures?

That introspection is how this book started. If you read the daily news and feel compassion for people great and small; if you long to increase the meaning of your life by helping repair what is wrong in the world; if you are haunted by the questions, What can I do? How can I help?, then this book is for you. If you feel you are nobody special and wonder what you can give that will matter—it turns out, you can offer quite a bit.

The great religious and philosophical traditions in the world all have teachings that treating others with the same weight and love with which we regard ourselves is the path to peace and enlightenment—do unto others as you would have done unto you. This universal value is called the Golden Rule. The Golden Rule can take on many other names or labels—compassion, community development, ministering, humanitarian work, neighborhood unity, disaster response, loving thy neighbor—but at its root is this simple yet demanding invitation: Treat even your enemy the way you want to be treated.

I have come to know that the principles behind *how* I am helping make a difference to the outcomes. I tell a lot of stories in this book, and I hope what you take away from reading them are the principles at work in those stories. They are not always intuitive, and it might take thirty years of making mistakes and miscalculations to know how true they really are. I also hope as you read that you will find touchstones for *why* you personally want to help others. What is your personal Golden Rule for your own life and times?

Understanding and applying these principles can be like red knitted slippers or a new pair of socks. They transform what could feel like a paltry offering into the right contribution given at the right time. They translate an everyday object into a love letter of human connection and caring. These are the secrets to doing small things with great love.

So I hope you read the first chapters and then help write the next chapters yourself. This is a work that belongs to all of us.

The Golden Rule[1]

- Baha'i: "Blessed is he who prefers his brother to himself" (Bahà'u'llàh tablets—19th century).

- Buddhism: "Whatever is disagreeable to yourself, do not do unto others" (The Buddha, Udana-Varga 5.18—6th century BC).

- Confucianism: "Do not do to others what you do not want them to do to you" (Confucius, Analects 15.23—5th century BC).

- Christianity: "You shall love your neighbour as yourself. On these two commandments depend all the Law and the Prophets" (Gospel of Matthew 22, 36-40—1st century AD).

- Gandhi: "To see the universal and all-pervading Spirit of Truth face-to-face, one must be able to love the meanest of all creation as oneself" (translated from *Il mio credo, il mio pensiero*, Newton Compton, Rome 1992, 70—20th century).

- Hinduism: "This is the sum of duty. Do not unto others that which would cause you pain if done to you" (Mahabharata, 5, 1517—15th century BC).
- Islam: "None of you will believe until you love for your brother what you love for yourself" (Hadith 13, The Forty Hadith of Imam Nawawi—7th century).
- Jainism: "In happiness and sorrow, in joy and in pain, we should consider every creature as we consider ourselves" (Mahavira, 24th Tirthankara—6th century BC).
- Judaism: "What is hateful to you, do not do to your fellow-man. This is the entire Law, all the rest is commentary" (Talmud, Shabbat 3id—16th century BC).
- Haudenosaunee Confederacy: "Respect for every form of life is the foundation" (The Great Law of Peace—16th century).
- Plato: "I can do to others what I'd like them to do to me" (5th century BC).
- Seneca: "Treat your inferiors as you would be treated by your betters" (Letter 47 11—1st century).
- Shintoism: "Be charitable to all beings, love is the representation of God" (approximately AD 500: Ko-ji-ki Hachiman Kasuga—8th century BC).

- Sikhism: "I am a stranger to no one, and no one is a stranger to me. Indeed, I am a friend to all" (Guru Granth Sahib, religious scripture of Sikhism, p. 1299—15th century).
- Voltaire: "Put yourself in the other person's shoes" (*Letters on the English*, n. 42).
- Yoruba wise saying (West Africa): "If somebody stings a bird with a sharp stick, should be first try it on himself and realise how badly it hurts" (collected in 1985 after many centuries of oral traditions).
- Zoroastrianism: "Do not do to others what is harmful for yourself" (Shayast-na-Shayast 13, 29—between 18th and 15th century BC).

CHAPTER 1

The Basics

1

There is an innate desire in most of us to take something wrong and make it right. But good intentions often, ironically, fail. Why? Sometimes, subconsciously, it was more about us than it was about them. It's easy to seek for that quick emotional high that comes from fixing an intractable problem, but it's often more complicated than we thought it was going to be. Maybe we didn't recognize at the beginning the deeper, unmet needs or the realities people are facing. Perhaps it grew messy and out of control. There are so many unintended consequences.

Ernesto Sirolli tells a funny story about unintended consequences:[1]

> Everything I do professionally—my life—has been shaped by seven years of work as a young man in Africa.

From 1971 to 1977 . . . I worked in Zambia, Kenya, Ivory Coast, Algeria, [and] Somalia. I worked for an Italian NGO and every single project that we set up in Africa failed. And I was distraught. I thought—age 21—that we Italians were good people, and we were doing good work in Africa. Instead, everything we touched, we killed.

Our first project . . . was a project where we Italians decided to teach Zambian people how to grow food. So, we arrived there with Italian seeds in southern Zambia in this absolutely magnificent valley going down to the Zambezi River and we taught the local people how to grow Italian tomatoes and zucchini. And of course, the local people had absolutely no interest in doing that so we paid them to come and work and sometimes they would show up.

And we were amazed that the local people, in such a fertile valley, would not have any agriculture. But instead of asking them how come they were not growing anything, we simply said, "Thank God we [are] here, just in the nick of time to save the Zambian people from starvation." And of course, everything in Africa grew beautifully. We had these magnificent tomatoes. In Italy a tomato would grow to this size, in Zambia to *this* size.

4

And we could not believe [it]. We were telling the
Zambians: look how easy agriculture is!

When the tomatoes were nice and ripe and
red—overnight some 200 hippos came out from
the river, and they ate everything! And we said to
the Zambians, "The hippos!" And the Zambians
said "Yes, that's why we have no agriculture here."
"Why didn't you tell us?" "You never asked."

I thought it was only us Italians blundering
around Africa but then I saw what the Americans
were doing, what the English were doing, what the
French were doing. And after seeing what *they*
were doing I became quite proud of our project
in Zambia. Because you see at least we fed the
hippos!

Sirolli's story is humorous, but this scenario plays out
every day someplace in the world. Good intentions don't
ensure good outcomes. Helping other people is both an
art and a science. At its best, it can also be a personal expression of solidarity when we each exchange our offerings
with skill and compassion. There are critical principles that
can ground us in the best lessons learned over time.

But before the principles can be fully understood,
there are some basic truths that make up the bedrock
foundation. For me, these truths are like five steel beams
that undergird my personal learnings about helping in

ways that last, have impact, and dignify others instead of making them new victims of my good intentions.

These five basic truths help explain why the principles are right and powerful:

- Universal human rights
- The fundamentals of humanitarian action
- Infusing service with sincere love
- The chance to build character in givers and receivers
- The fatherhood of God for the human family

1. Universal Human Rights

In the middle of the twentieth century, after the brutality of the two world wars, there was a great interest among nations to find better ways to promote peace and protect human rights. In 1946, each country sent delegates to the newly formed United Nations. United States President Harry Truman invited former First Lady Eleanor Roosevelt to be part of the US delegation.

By that point, Eleanor Roosevelt had formidable experience and political skills, but she grew annoyed by the men in the delegation who tried to keep her out of their main conversations. When it came time to join the committee that ultimately wrote the Universal Declaration of Human Rights, the male delegates believed the appointment would be more social than substantive. They had little interest and left the details to Eleanor. She became the chair of the United Nations Commission on Human Rights[2] and led the committee to produce one of the foundational texts in world history for human and civil rights law.

The committee successfully drafted the Universal Declaration of Human Rights largely because the individual members knew how to work together, negotiating different opinions into consensus. Eleanor Roosevelt's biographer, Blanche Wiesen Cook, describes that it was Mrs. Hansa Mehta, a delegate from India, who made the point that if the wording said: "'All men are treated free and equal around the world,' it will be all men—women not included." So the wording was changed to *all human beings*. That small adjustment had an enormous impact during the following decades. "All human beings—men and women and children—have these rights."[3]

The United Nations General Assembly accepted the Universal Declaration of Human Rights on December 10, 1948, and today, it has been signed by every one of the 192 member states of the United Nations. Its ratification was a significant moment in world history. Anyone interested in hoping to improve human circumstances through humanitarian aid, development, activism, or community service needs familiarity with these bedrock principles. Negative conditions arise because essential human rights are violated, and there is no remedy. The declaration gives a frame of reference for agreed-upon rights when people are under stress. Eleanor Roosevelt herself said that the real power is not in the document signed by nations, but in the hearts of people who believe it.

ELEANOR ROOSEVELT

"This universal declaration of human rights may well become the international magna carta of all men everywhere. . . . The real change, which must give to people throughout the world their human rights, must come about in the hearts of people. It is a declaration of basic principles of human rights and freedoms. And to serve as a common standard of achievement for all peoples of all nations. If we observe these rights for ourselves and for others, I think we will find that it is easier in the world to build peace."[4]

Look here for a deeper dive into the text of the Universal Declaration of Human Rights: https://shdwmtn.com/UN

The declaration lays out in simple language a common understanding of human dignity. Every person in any situation qualifies for human rights simply by being a human being. Infusing this understanding into my bones helped me recognize in my own work that the respect and dignity we accord each other does not and never has depended on geography, class, religious belief, gender, chance for learning, station, political persuasion, ethnicity, orientation, ability, or any other classification.

2. The Fundamentals of Humanitarian Action

After 100 years of experience and humanitarian work on the battlefield and in other emergencies, the Red Cross/Red Crescent movement announced in Vienna in 1965 that it would be governed by certain fundamental principles of humanitarian action.[5]

Humanity

Suffering requires a response; it cannot be met with indifference. All human beings have dignity and must be protected and helped regardless of who they are or what they have done.

Impartiality

People are helped regardless of their religious beliefs, color of skin, political convictions, geographic origin, financial status, or any other category. Decisions about whom to help must be made on a "needs only" basis and must not be influenced by personal considerations or feelings. The deciding factor in who is helped first is only those who are in the greatest need.

Neutrality

One cannot take sides in speech, action, time, or place. It is important to maintain dialogue with all sides in crisis or violence. Neutrality assures that help given will not interfere in the conflict. Neutral conduct in peacetime and earning the confidence of all sides helps keep neutral acts in times of conflict.

Independence

Assistance cannot be impartial and neutral if it is not independent. While supportive of governments and subject to the laws of respective countries, organizations must keep their autonomy so they can act in accordance with their principles. They must take care not to submit to any interference or pressure.

Voluntary Service

Voluntary service is not prompted in any manner by desire for gain or advantage. There is no motive for offering assistance other than a desire to help. This is a powerful statement of solidarity.

Unity

Service and assistance must be open to all and draw recipients, volunteers, and staff from all ethnic and social groups without any discrimination.

Universality

The universality of suffering requires a universal response. There exists a collective responsibility to assist one another in responding to crises and to support each other's development in a spirit of solidarity and mutual respect.

Not only are all national committees of the Red Cross and Red Crescent committed to following these principles, but the first four have also become the accepted gold standard for all credible humanitarian and service organizations.[6] These fundamental truths are important in my own work because they give guidance when circumstances are not ideal. Do war criminals have rights to receive help? Should my project become an instrument of the government?

3. Love in Action Is Service

When thinking about great service to the poor, Mother Teresa inevitably comes up. Originally from Macedonia and a Roman Catholic nun all her adult life, she spent seventy years serving people in India who were poor, outcast, sick, and dying. Her service was deeply rooted in her Christian faith, her love of God, and her devotion to His children on earth.[7]

One of her most influential premises was that no kind act is too small to contribute, and no person is too insignificant to be respected and loved. Though she was known around the world and won the Nobel Peace Prize in 1979, she lived in poverty herself and donated the cash from her Nobel Prize money to the care of the poor.

She had a way of imparting inspiration in short sentences, which makes her very quotable. Her wisdom inspires millions of others to demonstrate their faith by love. She was canonized by Pope Francis I on September 4, 2016. Here are twelve of her most famous quotes on serving others.[8]

- "Not all of us can do great things. But we can do small things with great love."
- "If you judge people, you have no time to love them."
- "The most terrible poverty is loneliness, and the feeling of being unloved."
- "God doesn't require us to succeed, He only requires that you try."
- "Prayer is not asking. Prayer is putting oneself in the hands of God, at His disposition, and listening to His voice in the depth of our hearts."

- "Do not wait for leaders; do it alone, person to person."
- "One of the realities we're all called to go through is to move from repulsion to compassion and from compassion to wonderment."
- "Live simply so others may simply live."
- "Never worry about numbers. Help one person at a time and always start with the person nearest you."
- "We must know that we have been created for greater things, not just to be a number in the world, not just to go for diplomas and degrees, this work and that work. We have been created in order to love and to be loved."
- "I used to believe that prayer changes things, but now I know that prayer changes us, and we change things."
- "Prayer in action is love, love in action is service."

What I appreciate most about Mother Teresa's ethos is that it is scaled so that anyone of any means or circumstance can do it. No one is kept away from accessing the most powerful force on earth if they only and without self-interest love another person.

4. Building Character in Givers and Receivers

The early years of the Great Depression in Salt Lake City, Utah, where I live, was a time of terrible economic stress and hopelessness. Families were out of work, hungry, competitive, angry, and in despair. They felt they were being ground up by the forces of the Great Depression, and their most important relationships were disintegrating.

Leaders of The Church of Jesus Christ of Latter-day Saints tried everything they could think of to relieve tens of thousands of people struggling financially and spiritually. At the same time, they were worried about the corrupting influence of handouts on the dignity and self-worth of individuals and families. In their writings, Church leaders were especially concerned about the effects of poverty and idleness on character.[9]

J. Reuben Clark Jr. was a prominent attorney in the US State Department and served as the Undersecretary of State in President Coolidge's administration. He was appointed as the US ambassador to Mexico in 1930. In 1933, he resigned as ambassador to serve full-time as a religious leader in The Church of Jesus Christ of Latter-day Saints during this critical time. His description of the long-term objective from those stressful days has become a touchstone for me. The rather old-fashioned language still rings with a certain clarity.

J. REUBEN CLARK JR.

"The real long-term objective of the welfare plan is the building of character in . . . givers and receivers, rescuing all that is finest down deep inside of them and bringing to flower and fruitage the latent richness of the spirit, which after all is the mission and purpose and reason for being of [Christ's] church."[10]

Character seems like a funny point to be troubled about during an economic meltdown, but these leaders were consumed by the idea that dependency would dismantle dignity and self-worth and that children living through the emergency would not learn work if their only hope was receiving aid.

My own definition of character is the daily seed of energy an individual expends to grow productively in a good direction. Over time, the growth matures into a sapling and then a young tree. That daily energy spent for good blooms and then ripens into consistent behavior. The tree is acknowledged as belonging to an orchard, where the trees are not dependent so much as interdependent. Each tree contributes unique and valuable fruit, and the orchard nourishes the community. Character consists of *moral actions that take into account the improvement of the whole society and not just the individual.*

Givers, under the 1936 church welfare plan, deserved as much attention as receivers because inequality and stratification easily destroy respect and empathy. There are no givers without receivers. Every person is a giver and a receiver at the same time. There is a richness of spirit in each person that can be nurtured until it bears its unique fruit. Society is the wealthier for it.

The church leaders of that day crafted a system, and its centerpiece was engaging people and busying them in worthwhile activities so they could exchange what they had for what they needed. Every effort was acceptable, and everyone was helped. On the surface, it was about employment, but in reality, they were developing resilience, self-respect, and community networks that could sustain them through much longer crises. The aim was to concretely help people help themselves. They called the idea self-reliance.[11]

Here is an example of how that worked:

In 1930, farmers couldn't sell their crops for what it cost to harvest them. They were eating what produce they could and leaving the rest to rot in fields. At the same time, 60 percent of the working population in Salt Lake City was unemployed. Food prices were beyond the reach of out-of-work families.

One of the first projects involved negotiating an agreement with the farmers for the church to provide free labor in exchange for a percentage of the harvest. Hundreds of people rode trucks every day out to the farms. Storehouses popped up in vacant buildings so that different crops given as payment could be sorted and traded. A small cannery was built to preserve the produce for winter months. People with means purchased food from the storehouses, and the money was used to buy clothing and blankets for others. Those without means received groceries in exchange for volunteer labor geared toward their capacity. Ill people were cared for by families and neighbors using the resources of the storehouses. Farmers had farm labor, individuals had productive work, families had food, everyone had dignity.[12]

The men and women who began the Latter-day Saint welfare program were committed to the idea that each person needs dignified work and social connection. Every person needs to voluntarily choose their path and what they will give and do. Serving in the community binds everyone in a common cause. They preached thrift because they didn't want to waste anything or anyone.

More than ninety years later, the network of storehouses, canneries, farms, and thrift stores they started still thrives. People who need assistance and people who are giving assistance work shoulder to shoulder. Groceries, clothing, furniture, and household goods are dispensed without any money being exchanged. The founding principles taught in the 1930s still inform the humanitarian program I help administer today. Particularly, learning to respect the choices of others and safeguarding dignity have changed the way I work.

- Choice
- Thrift
- Work
- Service
- Dignity
- Friendship

I believe these same principles should be just as compelling today. Whatever the crisis, the opportunity for dignified work, personal growth, and community connection will rescue all that is finest inside each person.

5. The Fatherhood of God, the Love of Jesus Christ

One of the simplest and most moving of all religious ideas is that we are all children of God. We may worship differently, but the fatherhood of God makes us literally siblings. God made us different on purpose and with great variety.

Jesus Christ taught a radical gospel. It was designed to move people past selfish self-interest to the undeniable truth that all humanity is one big web. We are connected to one another as extensively as the whole earth and as intimately as family. If someone takes your coat, give them your cloak also. If they compel you to walk a mile, walk two. Blessed are the merciful. Blessed are the peacemakers. Love God with all your heart, might, mind, and strength. Give evidence of that love by loving your neighbor. On these unintuitive ideas hangs everything else.

I sometimes hear the question of why an all-powerful God would allow so much evil and suffering in the world. It strikes me as an uncomfortably passive inquiry. For me, the compelling question is, Why do we as children of an all-powerful God—who has given us strict and holy commandments to love one another—permit so much evil and suffering in the world He gave us to run? I know that other people's bad choices are creating pain far beyond my ability to influence, but I ask myself, What can I do individually and collectively about the things I hate in this world? If we really are agents to act and not be acted upon, then what am I prepared to do?

The simple, deep Christian answer to that question is distilled in twenty-six mostly one-syllable words:

"As I have loved you, . . . love one another.
. . . By this shall all men know that ye are

my disciples, if ye have love one to another" (John 13:34–35).

The rest of the chapters in the book are principles drawn from my own experience. But I'm also interested in what you yourself have learned. Your experiences are as valid as anyone else's.

Questions To Consider

- What are the steel beams that have been the most important in your own life?

- What do you know about helping in ways that last?

- Why would an understanding of human rights be so critical before engaging in help or service?

CHAPTER 2

You Are Most Powerful Where You Live

2

I have a recurring dream that chokes me with fear and adrenaline. A soot-colored tide surges through palm trees skirted in ruffles of white water. A wave greedily devours neat rows of greenhouses and races on unsatisfied and ravenous across the land. It barrels toward the railroad track and the daily train to Galle. The rusty red train cars have large windows. Women in colored saris lean out of the windows, accepting children into their arms and setting them down inside the train. Panicked farmers hand up more toddlers as the water rises. Surely the train on the high track will be the safest place. Then the greedy wave eats up the farmers and slams the train over and over in the violent surf until it tumbles and floods. In the dream, the bodies of women with their saris covering their faces float out the windows like a parade.

In this dream, I am powerless. I stand paralyzed and mute, unable to do anything or save anyone. The dream flows from a real experience, and the fact that it is still in my subconscious reveals how much the encounter changed me.

In the aftermath of the 2004 catastrophic Southeast Asia tsunami, I went to Sri Lanka with a project to help fishermen and seamstresses get new work tools so they could go back to providing for their families. Every community we entered was filled with dank debris and people still deep in shock five months after the tragedy.

When we came to the railroad tracks where the train to Galle met its end, there were families camped all around the broken train. We got out of the vehicle, and the driver, Shanthe, told me the story of what happened. I saw a white sheet tacked to the side of the train with writing painted on it, and Shanthe read to me: "We now understand the power of the sea because it took our children from us." People soon came up to me and plucked at my sleeve or held my hand and said the only English words they knew: "I lost my baby. I lost my husband. Help me. Please, please help me." I was at a loss. I didn't have any food to share. I couldn't speak their language to explain. I was in the country to try to help, but how could I tell them that fishermen were getting nets and boats and seamstresses were getting machines and cloth? Nine hundred houses were being built just over the rise from where we were, but what was that to them?

Shanthe went over to our vehicle and took out a soccer ball. Soon he was kicking it around with a mob of kids. They began to scuffle and laugh with him in the dirt. While he played with the ball, Shanthe casually asked one woman how her bread-making was turning out. She brought some bread for him to try. Another woman called to him that they couldn't find washing powder. He said he would try to find some for them.

Standing there watching the scene, I recognized something I had never understood before. Shanthe was more powerful than I was in this setting for very ordinary reasons. This was his home. He came consistently. He spoke the language. He understood the cultural dynamics. He could respond at a very personal, human level.

You are at your most powerful where you live.

It's such an important principle—you are most powerful where you live. When you first hear that statement, it's easy to think of all the reasons it isn't true. Your first instinct is to say, "My neighborhood doesn't need me the way they do in Ukraine or Sudan." But thinking it through, some realities are quickly evident. When it comes to making meaningful contributions to disasters that are far away, we are limited by distance, time, security, and knowledge. You might go to all the effort and expense to cross the ocean and arrive at the site of the disaster only to be turned away because it is too insecure for civilians or because your presence is attracting negative attention or because you are taking up desperately needed food, water, and shelter from the people you are trying to help. Even if you find a niche where you can do something useful, you will stay for a week or two and then be gone again. These are the limitations.

The next thought is, "Well, the least I can do is send things they need." It can be emotionally satisfying to think of something we are sure the people will need in their extremity and then go to great lengths to gather and transport it. We are expending our energy commensurate to the scale of the disaster and to our empathy. But goods donated in a time of disaster can go horribly wrong. Let me give some examples.

In 1998 Hurricane Mitch blasted with fury across Honduras. Eleven thousand people died, and more than a million and a half people were left homeless. *CBS* Sunday Morning interviewed Juanita Rilling, who was the director of the Center for International Disaster Information in Washington, DC. She related, "[I] got a call from one of our logistics experts who said that a plane full of supplies could not land, because there was clothing on the runway. It's in boxes and bales. It takes up yards of space. It can't be moved. 'Whose clothing is it?' He said, 'Well, I don't know whose it is, but there's a high-heeled shoe, just one, and a bale of winter coats.' And I thought, winter coats? It's summer in Honduras."[1]

In humanitarian circles, the tidal wave of unusable donations that clogs up the logistics is called *the second disaster*. Rilling also describes how, in 2004, following the Indian Ocean tsunami, a beach in Indonesia was piled high with used clothing that had been sent from abroad. There was no time for disaster workers to sort through and clean the old clothes to make them usable, so the contributions sat on the beach in the tropical sun, rotting. The huge pile became a toxic hazard, and there was no choice but to destroy it. "Local officials poured gasoline on it and set it on fire. And then it was out to sea."[2]

These are shocking stories, but the "second disaster" is the reality in so many emergency settings.

Dale Herzog is a logistical and supply chain engineer at the UPS Foundation. He tells of his experience in Sandy Hook after the 2012 elementary school shooting tragedy:

> Thousands of boxes of Christmas toys, school supplies, gifts and clothing were sent to Newtown, Connecticut, along with over half a million cards, letters and paper snowflakes. Something like 65,000 teddy bears were mailed there, more than 1,000 of them life-sized. It was a tremendous gesture of love from people around the world, but the logistical challenges presented by these gifts stretched residents to the breaking point. Newtown is a small, semi-rural town made up of villages, with a total population of just 27,000. With its limited postal resources, many other public employees—EMS, police, firefighters—and volunteers from surrounding post offices had to be brought in to handle all the stuff. At one point, the donations occupied 80,000 square feet of floor space stacked tightly together and standing eight feet high. During a time in which their community was struggling with unbearable grief, residents were forced to worry about what to do with this avalanche of packages, letters and cards.[3]

His words sound brutal and uncaring, but they reflect a reality that has become disconnected from our good intentions. The gestures of goodwill offerings can simply be physically overwhelming.

Dale shares a second story that occurred after the 2010 Haiti earthquake:

> "There was the company that sent ten full shipping containers of refrigerators—hundreds of fridges—to Haiti after the 2010 earthquake. It may sound generous, until you realize that most of the survivors were living in tents without electricity *and* none of the appliances were wired to work in that country."[4]

Early in my career, my organization routinely shipped hygiene kits and medical supplies by ocean container to support different projects. Community groups would donate the equipment or assemble the kits, and then we would box and label them, load them onto pallets, and ship them across the ocean in forty-foot containers. The transit usually took eight weeks, and each container cost between $6,000 and $8,000. A large portion of my job was negotiating with customs officials in the ports who were holding the shipments for legitimate (or sometimes nonlegitimate) reasons to get the containers released.

Sometimes, we paid large storage fees until the containers were cleared. Other times, the difficulties could not be resolved, and the shipment had to be abandoned or shipped back. Very often, by the time the containers arrived at their destinations, we had spent more money getting them on location than the contents were worth inside.

In light of these experiences, we began exploring ways to purchase items locally and deliver them within a few days. Many believed it was still cost effective to receive higher-quality donations not available in local markets or that local purchases would discourage our volunteer base who assembled the kits, but I discovered otherwise. The equipment purchased locally was already calibrated with the right electrical plugs and voltage. And it also came with a warranty and a referral to a local technician if repairs were needed. We began directing interested volunteers toward more local opportunities that needed their expertise and, in the long run, the new practice proved to be much more sustainable than shipping in equipment from other countries.

Several years after making the strategic switch to local purchases, I stood in the shade of an Amman, Jordan, garden putting toothpaste and shampoo into bags with women from the local Presentation of Our Lord Greek Orthodox Church and Arabic language students from the university. These neighbors were assembling supplies to be delivered to the Zaatari Syrian refugee camp. The mood was festive. They had done some hard bargaining in the local souk to get good prices for the supplies, with etiquettes I could not begin to understand. Vendors were happy, the neighborhood volunteers were enjoying getting to know each other, and everyone hoped the Syrians crossing the border in the next few days would feel relief receiving the needed items. I remember thinking that this project cost one-third the price of a shipping container, it rallied neighbors who didn't traditionally interact to an enjoyable afternoon activity, the contents would be familiar to the recipients, the camp officials would receive what they had requested, and it was to be distributed the next day at the border.

Dale recommends asking three questions before collecting and shipping humanitarian items:[5]

1. *"Is this stuff wanted?"* Have the people on the ground decided what is necessary and in which order it should arrive?
2. *"How will this stuff get there?"* And who will pay the cost?
3. *"How will the stuff get distributed after it arrives at its destination?"*

Those are very simple questions that delve right into the heart of the practical realities of location, and many people answering those questions will make a pivot toward cash as a more flexible and useful donation in a disaster. It is nearly always preferred by the agencies working on the ground. Cash is nimble, it supports vendors in the local economy, it can be quickly deployed elsewhere when the situation changes. But it can also seep away in corruption and be hard for donors to track. Credible organizations have robust ways of tracking and reporting where the cash goes. When you want to help in a specific situation, it's critical to know these realities and the unintended consequences so you can determine your best move.

It may be a hard truth that we cannot do much in conflict or disaster zones far away besides donate money to organizations who are on the ground, but there is much that we can do in our own towns that will change lives. It is a myth that you are more needed in Dar es Salaam than you are in Des Moines, Iowa. The problems are simply different. Shanthe was powerful because he was consistently present, he spoke the language, he understood and interpreted cultural cues, and he could build trusted relationships of encouragement—something that no amount of money can do.

Let me share some additional stories about others like Shanthe who created powerful relief because they possessed invaluable local tools.

Consistently Present

In a city just south of where I live, a woman lost her husband in an unexpected accident. She had three young children and very little means to support them. She was filled with grief and paralyzed by despair. She received a donation to help her finish her education, but there were many other barriers. One day, not long after the funeral, an older woman from the neighborhood came to the woman's home and told her, "I don't have any money to give you, but I have time. I will come each day and watch the children while you go to school." The two agreed on a plan, and five days a week, this good woman came each morning. While the widow went to the local university full-time, the older woman helped get the children ready for school, drove them where they needed to be, helped them with their homework, and made a hot meal for the evening—for two years. More than a babysitter, she became the wise, confident friend the family needed as they mourned the absence of their father and husband. It took enormous, consistent commitment and a suspension of her own activities by this woman, but it forever changed the lives of four other people.

Speak the Language

Speaking the language can be broader than the local dialect.

Vesta Stoudt created a household tool and saved lives because she spoke "navy." In 1943, Vesta's two sons were both serving in the navy during World War II, and she was working in an ordnance plant near Amboy, Illinois. Her job was to inspect rifle cartridges packed into boxes. After the inspection, the boxes were taped closed with a thin paper tape and then dipped in wax to make them waterproof for the damp conditions in the field. To open the box, soldiers would pull on the tab of tape, and it was supposed to rip through the wax, but the paper tape was not strong enough and often broke off, leaving the soldiers to claw open the box of ammunition under enemy fire.[6]

Vesta understood this flaw was putting lives at risk, including her sons', so she put her ingenuity to work. She experimented combining cotton duck cloth with glue and designed a strong, waterproof tape that met the field requirements.

Her samples impressed the military inspectors, but she could not get the supply chain in the military to change to the new tape. So Vesta wrote to the commander in chief. When President Franklin Delano Roosevelt received her energetic letter that included sketches of the problem, he contacted the War Production Board in Washington,

DC. Shortly, Vesta had a letter saying her recommendation for the new tape had been approved.

Johnson & Johnson, already making surgical tape for the military, received the contract to manufacture Vesta's idea, and they called it Duck Tape because it was waterproof, like a duck, and it was made with cotton duck fabric.

Vesta saw a specific need and responded, but she was effective because she understood the difficulties of the soldiers in the field and spoke the language of the military bureaucracy. She positioned her idea in the chain of command to quickly get it where it could do the most good.

Cultural Expertise

Milton Collins is the principal of Lincoln Elementary School in South Salt Lake. The year I visited him, he had students from fifteen countries enrolled. The Hamed brothers from Syria had just arrived in the city and were at the school on the first day. They were visibly nervous and very unsure about how they would be received. Principal Collins greeted them and their mother in the hall. He made sure the brothers had a backpack with the supplies they would need that day from the closet. He told the boys high fives were mandatory whenever they saw him in the hall. He directed them to go straight to an adult if they had a question or experienced bullying of any kind.

Milton Collins's job was to be a principal, but he went beyond his job to be a cultural guide for students on a day when guidance was badly needed. He knew he could be an unforgettable force for good in the lives of kids who had experienced bombs, hunger, death of loved ones, uncertainty, and now fear over whether they would fit in on the first day of school.[7]

Whenever there is a problem, the first thing Principal Collins does is invite everyone to meet face-to-face. His experience is that unintended cultural misunderstandings get in the way, and problems can't be sufficiently ironed out over email or phone calls. Milton says, "We gotta talk. Emails and text messages are completely different from face-to-face. The only way we fix it is to sit down and have a conversation. . . . Every kid is one caring adult away from being a success story."[8]

Trusted Relationships of Encouragement

I met Janet Hatch in 2023 in my neighborhood. She had been a beloved first-grade teacher for many years while she'd raised her four children as a single mom. A failed back surgery created an intense pain-feedback loop that confined her to her bed or recliner. She described it as a full-body spasm that never let go. Janet knew her life would be cut short. She loved family history and had so many stories inside her head that she wanted to share with her grandchildren. She tried dictation apps, but her voice wasn't strong enough for the app to work well. She tried having friends come type for her, but they weren't always available when she had the energy. She intensely wished she could do it herself, but she had only enough strength to type on her iPad for about fifteen minutes each day.

She was feeling sorry for herself and her dreams when a voice inside her head said, "Just start." In the brief ten to fifteen minutes she had each day, Janet wrote twenty-three books. They were bound and spread out on her coffee table, filled with her insights and photos, memories and wisdom. Janet knew she wouldn't leave much of an inheritance, but she distilled all her inner wealth—in fifteen-minute increments—into an individual book for each member of her family, describing how she felt about their births and reassuring them for their futures. She finished the last book for her as-yet unborn granddaughter and then passed away, having given a powerful gift of specific, personal encouragement that no one else could give.

Of course it is harder to work where you live. It's harder because we understand the dynamics and real barriers that may be invisible to us in unfamiliar cultures and places.

Are there exceptions? Absolutely. Carefully organized, self-sufficient groups who come at a requested time into a disaster area to help clean up or rebuild can be a boon to the affected community. But the exceptions prove the rule.

What about organized humanitarian trips and travel? It's important to recognize what a trip can and cannot accomplish. A foreigner spending a limited amount of time in a village cannot expect to spark structural change that reduces poverty. But expanding the person's worldview and empathy is not insignificant. Trips can definitely be about connection, learning, and exchange. They can be especially important for young people who are developing empathy and forming opinions about the world, but they can easily slip into inadvertent patronizing, which makes everybody poorer.

If you decide to participate in a humanitarian trip, ask yourself: How am I different because of this experience? What surprised me? Which skills do the people have that I don't? Do the issues that I observed on my trip exist in some form in my own community? What will I do differently now that I've made this trip? How will I keep the personal connection and friendships?

In the end, you yourself are the gift. It isn't the clothing, the hygiene kits, the school desks, or the wells. It's you. It's the connections and relationships you make. I envision each person as a well-stocked humanitarian organization, but instead of giving out tangible goods in foreign locations, we dispense as our humanitarian offerings the richness of healing, friendship, respect, peaceful dialogue, sincere interest, protective care for children, birthday remembrances, and taking care of the stranger right where we live. Anyone can do this type of humanitarian work at any time. It doesn't require warehouses or fundraising or transportation. You can be perfectly responsive to any need that comes to you wherever you are.

If we change our perspective so that caring for other people is less about giving things away and more about filling a hunger for human connection, holding meaningful conversations, and building rich, positive relationships, which doors would open to us? What suffering would be relieved?

Every person can live this kind of humanitarian life, but it takes vision and commitment to recognize the humanitarian opportunity at any moment of any day. Of course, some people may not respond positively to what you offer. There are always humanitarian places we cannot yet reach. But there are plenty we can reach.

We are most powerful where we live.

CHAPTER 3

Trusted Networks

3

Why aren't wealthy nations, corporations, and individuals spending more money to alleviate poverty? It's a legitimate question. But I ask myself if money is the determining factor in relieving poverty. By some estimates, the world has poured nearly $2 trillion into addressing chronic issues in Africa.[1] Why isn't the situation better? Money is certainly necessary, but I don't find it to be the determining factor for long-term success in humanitarian efforts.

Dambisa Moyo, an economist from Zambia, wrote the book *Dead Aid: Why Aid Is Not Working*. The book's premise is that Western nations' development aid to Africa—meant to alleviate poverty and jump-start economies—has instead unintentionally fostered dependency and corruption and made Africa poorer. This is a somewhat controversial position. Some good has certainly come from the long-term focus on African development—but many of the issues the development dollars are trying to address were caused or made worse by the incalculable amounts of money, resources, and human capital extracted from Africa over hundreds of years by colonizing forces. Money alone does not solve those problems. In the absence of ethical leadership, self-determination, and the protection of basic human rights, development aid has proved to do very little to change the reasons communities and countries are poor.[2]

What does work? The progress I have seen generally grows out of the presence of trusted networks that practice the mundane skills of inclusion, protecting alternate views, choice and accountability, and gathering everyday people for change. Money is critical, but it doesn't necessarily create those fundamentals. They must be developed alongside the resource, and frankly, it is much harder work. Without these additional elements, the money can inadvertently increase inequality, corruption, and prolonged conflict.

Trusted networks come in many forms—an extended family, a homeowners' association, a water committee, a parent-teacher-student association, a fraternity or sorority, a book club, a running group, a veterans' association, a school class, or an interfaith council. The presence of these groups doesn't mean they are trusted networks, but they each have the potential to be. A network becomes trusted when the members have confidence in each other and develop trustworthy cooperation under various stresses. One of the reasons religious communities and faith-based organizations can often act as powerful change agents is that they are inherently made up of overlapping trusted networks. They tend to be the structure in the community that knows everybody's name and circumstance. They don't come from the outside but are functioning where they live and have extensive grassroots reach. Many can also connect to other congregations or faith leaders in neighboring geographies to cooperate at scale.

What follows is an exploration of trusted networks and the elements that I believe help determine their success. Combined with financial resources, these ordinary acts done well can bolster thriving communities where people create their own progress.

Trusted Networks Are Inclusive

Everyone has something valuable to offer. Everyone is rich in some way, and the variety of that truth is what makes the world whole. Social networks—I mean actual people and not the digital version—that respect and incorporate a variety of offerings from their members become trusted networks that can effectively address problems.

I once had the responsibility to supervise an internship program that trained students from three universities and placed them in international settings to teach an employment course for six months. One of the universities had consistent problems with communication and logistics. After not making much progress, I finally flew to the campus and sat down with the coordinator, prepared to tackle the problems. I remember I had a yellow legal pad in my hand with six bullet points that I felt were critical to resolve.

The man was from Fiji and had a big personality and a warm handshake for me. He invited me into his office, where I promptly launched into the purpose of my visit. After I stopped to take a breath, he smiled and said, "Sister, we don't know each other. We have many things to talk about today. So let me get to know you a little bit. Tell me about your family. What is your story? Then I will tell you about mine. As we say in Fiji, we are going to 'talk story' for thirty minutes, and then we will discuss the internship program."

I stared at him in disbelief. Were we really going to chitchat about our backgrounds for thirty minutes? But he knew something I did not: It's much easier to resolve problems when there is a personal foundation of trust. I assumed he was doing his job poorly, but it turned out there were many factors I did not yet understand. "Talking story" gave us a chance to establish some foundational respect before resolving the six points on my legal pad.

It can be easy to dismiss people as incompetent or "not needed" when they don't live up to some invisible standard we have in mind. My coworker from Fiji helped me recognize that an individual with a drastically different outlook from my own is immensely valuable because of that difference. I was devaluing the very source I needed to solve the problem I faced.

Thrift is an old-fashioned word rarely used anymore, but it is the mindset that small amounts are still valuable and that small efforts, small coins, small bits of time, etc., can contribute to something much greater. In the New Testament, the widow's two mites humbly and without fanfare placed into the temple treasury were a product of both her thrift and her love. Jesus proclaimed it was worth "more than they all" (Luke 21:3).

Thrift can also be applied to relationships in the form of a belief that no one is too poor, too disabled, too marginalized, too street weary, or too anything else to contribute something of value to society. Even more than money and time, people are too precious to waste. Waste of any kind drains hope, and the waste of a human being's unique offering is a betrayal. So ask, Who isn't participating? How can the trusted network be enlarged so they can engage?

My colleague Elizabeth taught me a great lesson about not letting fear or discomfort prevent me from expanding the circle of my attention. I'll share a story to illustrate this point, though I've changed Marilyn's name to protect her privacy.

A woman begging outside my office building was a fixture for many years, but she didn't sit quietly with a cardboard sign or ask passersby for a bit of money. Her technique was to pop out of nowhere and follow the person very closely across the street, in their face, begging and haranguing, "Please. Help. Me. Please, please!" She surprised me often, and I will admit I many times used the entrance on the other side of the building because I didn't want to encounter her. I suppose she went beyond what I felt was the "polite" way of beggars.

So I was astonished when my coworker Elizabeth approached the woman and greeted her by name. "Marilyn, how are you today?!" Marilyn was suddenly transformed into a completely different being. She raised her head and responded that it was a good day because she had seen her high school–aged children on their way to school.

I asked Elizabeth, "How do you know her?" Elizabeth told me that she met Marilyn on the street, the same uncomfortable way I did. Elizabeth rarely gave money, but she and her husband, Mark, began offering Marilyn something more valuable: dignified attention. Most people hustled past Marilyn, and Marilyn usually kept her head down once they did. But Mark would call out her name, and recognizing his voice, she would look up to greet him.

She would give him the latest news about her daughter and son, and this allowed Marilyn to interact as a mother instead of as a panhandler. Marilyn's dream was to earn enough money to take the bus to Chattanooga, Tennessee. The poetry of the name Chattanooga is what drew her there.

When Elizabeth and Mark brought their family downtown at Christmas to see the lights, they introduced their daughters to Marilyn. Marilyn was obviously pleased and spoke animatedly with the girls. Marilyn produced a slice of red velvet cake she had saved for Mark as a Christmas gift. Mark protested, saying that just her friendship was enough, but Marilyn replied, "You talk to me, you are nice to me, and I want to give you something." The family returned home feeling very humble.[3]

I learned that Marilyn had hidden depth and generosity that I had known nothing about. I had categorized her only as a beggar and someone to avoid. I was walking every day into my office to work on helping marginalized people feel more belonging, and I failed to see the friendship and perspective Marilyn could offer me if I shared dignity and sincere caring with her.

Jesus Christ declared that the two most important behaviors—the two on which all others hang—are to love God with all our hearts and to love our neighbors as ourselves. A lawyer in the crowd quibbled and asked, "But who is my neighbor?" (Luke 10:29). And that prompted Jesus's parable of the Good Samaritan (see Luke 10:30–35). Of course, this parable is about people like me, who see an injured person on the road and pass by on the other side, and a Samaritan, who knew better what to do. The Samaritan understood that a neighbor is someone who needs a trusted network and doesn't have one.

Trusted Networks Protect Alternate Views

Networks that have worked to be inclusive will predictably contain subgroups or individuals who do not agree on all points or who may be in danger of being dominated by the majority view. Alternate opinions are important. Just because a view is held by the majority does not mean it is fully correct. Truth is scattered among us, and we each reflect reality and equity through the lens of our unique experiences. Trusted networks recognize that many views have merit and a place in considerations. Trusted networks strengthen when they adjust to accommodate alternate viewpoints.

Many questions immediately arise: What does it look like to accommodate and value alternate viewpoints? How does one solve inevitable conflicts? How does one lay the groundwork for respectful disagreement without conflict? What does one do when a trusted network is struggling?

I wish I knew the answers to these questions, but I do know a few key pieces that have helped me in my own quest to build trusted networks.

- The network needs a commitment to equality and constructive action.
- Leaders demonstrate by their own actions that different perspectives are welcome, valid, and relevant.
- Members practice direct but kind communication and don't allow back-channel conversations to damage the network.
- Members share their personal stories, struggles, experiences, and perspectives to deepen relationships in a safe setting.
- Respectful disagreement is healthy and can bring out overlooked points, but ways to discuss without harming relationships need to be agreed upon.
- Spreading out roles among the group builds empathy and understanding. Members can experience leadership, fellowship, power, influence, accountability, and decision-making and have greater understanding when others fill those roles.
- Apologize, forgive, and fix mistakes quickly and with generosity.

Pamela Atkinson, the indefatigable Utah advocate for the unhoused, puts these bullets into practice this way.

"I never, ever let issues interfere with relationships. If a legislator said, 'Pamela, I'm not going to do it and this is why,' I say, 'You know, I really appreciate you sharing your thoughts with me and listening to me. If there's other information I can get you, please let me know.' Sometimes the legislator will say, 'Does this mean we can still be friends?' Absolutely. I once told somebody, 'I disagree with you 75 percent of the time, but I still like you and still learn from you.' You shouldn't dislike somebody because you disagree on certain issues."[4]

Few acts are as bonding as when members of one viewpoint stand up for the rights of another viewpoint. A good example is a story my friend Raad Kelani, a respected attorney in Amman Jordan, told me.

He related that when the Ottoman Empire ruled Jordan in the early twentieth century, the regime decided to collect taxes specifically from Christian citizens living in the cities of Salt and Karak. In preparation, a scout was sent to mark Christian houses so the tax employee would know from where to collect. The Muslim neighbors took exception to this act. That night, they also marked their own houses with the same mark. This confused the tax collectors, who could not tell which houses were Muslim and which were Christian. The whole population of the town stood together saying, "We are all brothers. If you intend to tax the Christians, you must tax us all."[5]

It may be an apocryphal story, but the idea of it is right.

My colleague Robert Hokanson, who visited the Jesuit Refugee Services office in Uganda, described a similar situation.

> "Most of the refugees from South Sudan are not Christian but are participating in food, rent, and job training programs that Jesuit Refugee Services sponsors. I sat down with a group receiving services. One of the families was a Muslim single father with two little girls. He told me: 'I love this place. It's the one place I can walk into and know I won't be discriminated against because I'm a Muslim.' I thought to myself, The one place is Jesuit Refugee Services? That example . . . is an extraordinary contribution to democracy, peace, and dignity for vulnerable families."[6]

Networks that have worked hard to be inclusive and to encompass a rich offering of viewpoints are in a good position to also foster a large array of choices for the community.

Trusted Networks
Foster Choices

I watched families in frigid weather select warm coats from a 100-pound bale that had been delivered. A girl about ten years old looked through the offerings until she found a pink sleeve. She pulled on it, and out came a fuzzy, fake-fur jacket. She immediately put it on, her face shining. It wasn't very practical for the cold weather; it came only to her waist, but she was delighted with her choice and would have no other. I've thought about this scene many times and how tightly the girl held on to that coat. One of the frustrating elements of living through crisis is how choices become severely limited. Besides the enormous injustice of having life and futures disrupted by the big event, people very often can no longer choose what they eat, where they live, whom they live next to, or what they wear. Options are many times predetermined by the agencies or governments helping them. Over time, this lack of choice provokes one of two reactions: Groups become either passive and no longer dream of acting on their own priorities, or they become agitated and confrontational, looking to stir up more options.

If the goal is to keep people in a position to act and not be acted upon, increasing choice turns out to be as critical as the available cash. Choice is one of the reasons emergency relief agencies have moved increasingly toward using preloaded cash cards and vouchers instead of preselected commodities.

The International Rescue Committee (IRC) delivers humanitarian aid in fifty countries and has worked for ninety years in some very fragile and low-resourced settings. Cash tools are becoming increasingly important in the IRC's programming. Stefano Battain is the deputy director of cash and markets for the IRC and explains why cash and vouchers help protect choices for families.

> "When people receive cash assistance, they are completely free to establish their own priorities. Not only choosing if they want to buy food, water, or go to the hospital but also deciding what kind of food they are buying for example. This is more dignifying and also has the advantage of contributing to the local economy."[7]

I admit, I was skeptical. The concern has always been that individuals would spend cash for nonessential items, leaving more vulnerable individuals still without food, or that corruption would disrupt the objectives. But evidence from more than thirty independent studies is compelling and has persuaded me that cash forms of humanitarian assistance can often empower choice and allow recipients to decide what their most pressing needs are and how they want to meet them. That is, after all, what I would want for myself.

One of these reports concludes: "In most contexts, humanitarian cash transfers can be provided to people safely, efficiently, and accountably. . . . Especially when delivered through digital payments, cash is no more prone to diversion than in-kind assistance."[8]

This doesn't mean I blithely recommend always giving cash when trying to help someone make a transformation, but I do acknowledge that flexible inputs support choices, and choice is an important consideration. If the person making the choices belongs at some level to a trusted network who can advise and consult, the chances of the constructive use of the money skyrockets. Trusted networks not only foster choice but also increase the likelihood of beneficial choices.

Trusted Networks Hold Themselves and Others Accountable

Trusted networks are key to allowing the money to do what it is intended to do. A large portion of effective poverty alleviation in the world is accomplished because of these networks. However, corruption will thwart the best intentions and siphon off goodwill into uncaring and greed. It rots trusted networks from within and destroys their ability to act effectively. For these reasons, it is imperative that trusted networks hold each other accountable.

There is a poignant passage in Isaiah in which the prophet, in the name of the Lord, holds the princes and ancient leaders accountable for their corruption: "Ye have eaten up the vineyard; the spoil of the poor is in your houses. What mean ye that ye beat my people to pieces, and grind the faces of the poor? saith the Lord God of hosts" (Isaiah 3:14–15).

I have thought hundreds of times about the phrase "the spoil of the poor is in your houses." I know that I am accountable to the ordinary people whose offerings fund the work I do each day. I have lain awake worrying about whether my mistakes will corrupt what has been given so freely. Many others are accountable with me, and it comforts me to know my trusted network is working together to avoid corrupting influences.

People are accountable when they take ownership for the actions and results of an effort. The accountable party ultimately answers for the completed objectives and reports back to the group on the commitments made. Mistakes inevitably arise, but accountable groups transparently work through the issues.

I know of a new Imam who was installed at a mosque that served a community where refugees had settled. He was a fiery speaker who began teaching anti-Christian sentiments. The older and respected Muslim residents of the town, rather than standing back and simply tolerating the approach, intervened and had the Imam corrected and ultimately replaced. They would not tolerate that kind of speech about their diverse neighbors in their community.

These are just a few examples of how trusted networks can hold each other accountable and prevent rifts and conflict in a community.

Trusted Networks Can Form Councils That Act

The most consistent activity that I participate in as a humanitarian is gathering a small group of motivated individuals from a trusted network, encouraging them to form a group to take concrete action, and supporting them as they act to prompt change. The name I give that small action group is a council. The council takes on a leadership role for the trusted network and works out the wrinkles to bring additional benefits to the group.

I recently sat with a nutrition council whose top concern was the children in their community who seemed underweight and sickly. They decided the first step was to organize a free screening to know specifically which children needed additional support. On a planned day, parents brought their children to be weighed and measured, but the crowd outside the doors was chaotic. The council member with the assignment to organize the line had underestimated the support they needed. He apologized and recruited volunteers to entertain children waiting for their turn. Others recognized the problem and undertook to escort families to the various rooms so the screening flowed in an orderly and kind way. Members of the council had arranged with the local government to send a nurse so that children who were in danger could receive immediate care, but she did not arrive. Phone calls revealed the buses had stopped running because of the rain. One of the council members was dispatched to fetch the nurse by car. Some parents from outside the community brought their children to the screening. There was a discussion among the council that it was unfair for these additional people to disrupt the day for those who had made appointments, but they agreed that they could be accommodated if the families were willing to wait until the end.

Many other problems and solutions transpired over the course of the day. The council sat in satisfied exhaustion when the event concluded. It had been a long day of work, but they had identified six children who were in serious health danger and ensured they were receiving care. The council felt the pride of strengthening their community. They felt accountable for the outcomes. Money was required to buy the screening equipment, pay for the nurse's time, purchase the healthy snacks, and pay for the therapeutic food some families received. But no amount of money could replicate the shared leadership of those community members working together to solve problems. The money was filtering through the work of the council for successful outcomes. Corruption was avoided because the council held themselves and others accountable.

Here is a summary of some of the best practices councils can follow.

10 Best Practices for Councils

- A leader facilitates, organizes, invites, and ensures all are heard, seeks clarity, identifies consensus, gives assignments, and asks for accountability—but the person is not in charge and not the ultimate decision-maker.
- All members have equal voice and share responsibility for the actions of the council.
- Alternate views are protected and encouraged.
- Kindness and respect mark discussions. Frankness and a lack of defensiveness are necessary.
- Driving a personal agenda is not acceptable.
- Rubber stamping ideas is unhelpful and undermines the process.
- Counseling takes time and deserves time to get it right.
- Assignments are given, and accountabilities are asked for.

- When all feel the energy of a discussion and decision, the council should act.
- The council is at its most powerful when it can act with genuine unanimity.

I lived for a year in a household with an eight-year-old named Sam, who was obsessed at the time with Lego Bionicle Toa. Toa are action figures that represent a fictional race of biomechanical beings with heroic powers and weapons.[9] Elaborate backstories had been written about their politics, moral code, genealogy, and destiny, and Sam knew every detail. As we walked along the city streets, Sam would quiz me on the properties of each Toa and exasperatedly correct me when I mixed them up. One thing Sam and I agreed on during those walks was the superiority of a certain Toa whose power was the ability to turn enemies into friends. That struck us as the ultimate superpower.

When trusted networks begin to form and support councils and those councils have at least some of the capabilities I have written about, they are poised to gather for action and change. Their ability to counsel with each other about specific issues and implement an action plan is a societal superpower. And under the right circumstances, it just might be one of the few forces that can turn enemies into friends.

I started this chapter with the unintuitive idea that money isn't the determining factor for charitable success. I don't want to give the impression that money isn't important. Enormous, sincere good comes from generous donors with significant resources who give money to address problems large and small. Good humanitarian organizations recognize and foster trusted networks. They should be able to demonstrate to donors and others how the trusted networks are functioning in the programs they fund. But I hope I have made the case that lasting change comes as money and other resources percolate through the protective filter of trusted networks.

Questions to Consider

- What trusted networks do you feel you belong to?

- In your experience, what prevents councils from falling apart into factions?

- Do you agree that cash is a legitimate option to increase choice in disaster settings?

- What best practices would you add to the list for high-functioning councils?

- When you donate money, what questions will you ask?

CHAPTER 4

Asking the Right Questions

4

My Solution to Your Problem Will Always Be Wrong

When I was first hired as the director of humanitarian services, I was young and green. My second-in-command was an old hand named Patrick Reese. He was thirty-six years into his career at this point and could have easily believed I knew too little and was too inexperienced to do the job, but he proved to be a good counselor. Patrick was a conscientious student of humanitarian principles and practice, and he generously shared his learnings with me.

Each morning, he would sit in my office for a few minutes and help me figure out what was important for the day and how to approach our tasks. He refused to get riled up by bureaucratic drama. He took a very long view. He didn't preach at me. He didn't remind me that he could do my job in his sleep. He listened to me and then repeated his mantra in those early morning sessions: "My solution to your problem will always be wrong. What do you think you should do?" He gave me confidence by sitting by my side and trusting me.

As Westerners, as people with resources, as graduates of higher education—we don't say it aloud but—our underlying attitude is so often that we know what is best for people, how to solve their problems—*we* will teach *them*. This never works. We have no idea what is best for people. We rarely know what is best for ourselves. We do not have the solution to their problems. We can listen, ask questions, share our stories, serve each other, be friends, ask a follow-up question, and try to bring forward helpful lessons. But the solutions to their problems lie inside them. Only they can find the answers. They are powerful where they live for all the reasons I wrote about in chapter 1.

In broad brushstrokes, there are five categories of questions that I think are useful when trying to help others think through a problem. They largely follow the pattern Patrick used to help me. Like Patrick did, our job is to listen and vigorously resist the temptation to rush to a solution.

One: What Help Do You Want?

When helping others work through a problem—the way Patrick did with me—asking questions is the way to begin. The very first thing to do is ask questions and really listen to the answers. Don't assume you know something. Your assumptions will derail you every time. Ask the people you are focused on serving: What's going on? Why is that happening? What have you tried? What happened when you tried that? What are you doing now? What do you wish you had? What do you want long-term? How can I help?

These aren't hard questions, but we get impatient and want to jump to the end.

The Pulitzer Prize–winning journalist Thomas L. Friedman wrote that asking questions and listening carefully is a profound signal to others of respect.

> The most useful lesson I learned as a journalist covering the Middle East on and off for some 45 years is to try to be a good listener. Because two things happen when I listen: One is that I learn when I listen. But much more important is what you say when you listen. That's because listening is a sign of respect.
>
> I found over the years that it was amazing what people would let me say to them, write about them or ask them about—if they thought that I respected them. And if they thought that I didn't respect them, I could not tell them the sky was blue. And the way they perceived

respect, first and foremost, was if you listened—not just waited for them to stop
talking—but deep listening. One can never
do that enough as a columnist, reporter,
or reader—especially today.[1]

Michael Nyenhuis, the very effective CEO of UNICEF
USA, told me a story he heard from a colleague:

They were working on health and had these
specific ideas about training health promoters
and establishing a community health post. Based
on all the work they had done elsewhere in the
region, it seemed like the right thing to do for this
community. They were meeting with the community leaders, and the leaders said, "We want
a soccer field for our kids." My colleague thought,
*Well, that won't work. This project is specifically
about community health.* The community per-
sisted. "We want to build a soccer field for kids . . .
with lights. That's what we really want. Our kids
need activity. Our kids need a place to play. Our
kids need to be safe in the evenings with lights
on the field. Our kids need a way to be in good
relationships with one another, to learn team-
work. We think having a decent place for them to
play soccer is the most important thing we can do
for their health." In the end, that team who was

trained to listen said, "All right. How can we help you do that?" They worked with the community to make it all happen. They found a grant to buy the lights. They built the soccer field. The community organized the sports.

For this community, the soccer field encompassed mental health, physical health, relational health, and safety. And later, they trained a health promoter and built a health post too. But it started by honoring the community's definition of health and their kids being active, which, if you think about the definition of health, is really what it means.[2]

Michael said the inverse is also true:

I visited an isolated rural community with a very nice health center. I was a little surprised to see it was built with a full surgical suite. I was there three years after it had opened, and the surgical suite had never been used because there were no surgeons anywhere nearby. It was overbuilt for the level of healthcare the community needed. So this surgical suite, paid for with donations and meant to be a help to the community, sat for three years without ever being used. The field of international humanitarian and development work is littered with projects that failed because there were good ideas developed by somebody from the outside who didn't take into account what the people in the communities where these things were going to be done actually wanted or needed.[3]

You may judge that asking and listening are the first steps in outlining a project, but that is skipping past the most important part: Asking and listening are the first steps in creating a relationship. The right tasks flow later, once the relationship is established.

Dr. James P. Comer is a gifted educator and one of the world's leading child psychiatrists. He is well known for his decades-long efforts to improve the school performance of children from lower-income and minority backgrounds.[4] Many years ago, I read one of his well-known quotes: "No significant learning can occur without a significant relationship."[5] Thinking back on my own experiences, I could see the truth in that statement. I have been most open to learning and changing when I have sensed that someone respected and cared about me more than just doing it for their job.

Carlton Ashby lives what Dr. Comer is describing. Mr. Ashby teaches kindergarten at Tarrant Elementary School in Hampton, Virginia. Tarrant is a Title 1 school in which 99 percent of the students receive a reduced or free lunch. The school's teachers are committed to the idea that they teach the whole child, not just a grade. Carlton tells this story about how the school faculty worked to create genuine relationships by listening to the parents and students before the school year started.

In the days before school started, our principal, Donna Warthan, hired two buses. The entire staff boarded those buses and rode into the neighborhood we serve. Armed with brochures about our school, we wandered the neighborhood. We rang doorbells. We sat on porches. We went into children's backyards. We dropped by corner stores. We visited playgrounds. All along the way, we shared how much we care about the children we teach. We shared the vision of success we hold for all our children.

The response to that simple gesture was both resounding and gratifying. Without exception, children and parents were excited that we took time to come and visit them in their neighborhood. We were the talk of the town!

Every day, I am reminded of how fortunate I am to teach at Tarrant Elementary. Our principal and teachers are committed to building relationships. . . . Every bit of success I [have] as a kindergarten teacher here . . . with 30 years of teaching experience, can be attributed to the fact that I care very deeply about building relationships with my students and with their parents, my colleagues, and our community.[6]

That image of those teachers getting in buses and visiting the homes of their students is vivid. They met the parents, asked what was important to them, ate a hot dog at the local store, or watched the kids playing basketball at the park. The sincere relationship each teacher initiated, even before the first day of school, put their students in a frame of mind to learn.

Asking and listening are premiere skills when trying to help another person.

Two: What Are You Able to Do Yourselves?

The next type of question seeks to discover what the person has already tried, what they are willing to do, and what things they want but feel might be beyond their abilities.

Mr. Gabriel was fifty-two years old, and this was his third time being a refugee. When he was a child, his family fled over the border to Ethiopia. The second time, he spent his college years in Kenya and qualified as a teacher. Now, he has been displaced a third time because of continuing conflict.

He crossed the border into Uganda with hundreds of thousands of others because it was not safe for them to remain. He looked around the refugee camp and saw thousands of children who were not in school, not learning. He knew they would soon fall hopelessly behind, and their formal education would be at an end—their futures limited.

He recognized other teachers whom he knew in the refugee population. There were no buildings, no supplies, no outside support—but they had knowledge and great desires for their children. Could they do something on their own?

He began organizing classes to meet under certain trees each day. A teacher gathered a group of students and gave lessons in the shade. They called them "Tree Schools," and Mr. Gabriel traveled among the trees, encouraging the teachers and helping them improve their skills in the unusual circumstances.

When I met him, he was teaching a class of 100 wiggly ten-year-olds. They were now assembled in a cement pavilion, but the kids still sat on the floor without any supplies. However, I was impressed with Mr. Gabriel. He did not wait for others to organize or for international agencies to help. His basic efforts allowed thousands of primary school children to keep learning through a very difficult displacement.

Mr. Gabriel is a champion. Every community has them. They are easy to recognize because circumstances cannot stop them. They start doing by using whatever is available, and their passion and energy attract additional help. When asked what type of help he would request, Mr. Gabriel surprised me. He said supplies would get quickly used up. What he wanted was more formal training for the teachers so they could manage the unusual circumstances and teach better lessons. He is a man of great vision. He is powerful because he himself overcame the barriers of getting his own education as a refugee, and he knows how to help others do the same. When you find a champion like Mr. Gabriel, who isn't waiting for others, I hope you move heaven and earth to help them in the ways they ask for.

Three: What Help Do You Want from the Community?

Jesse Hernandez was thirteen years old and playing with his cousins at Griffith Park in Los Angeles on Easter Sunday. The kids pushed on the door to an abandoned maintenance building, and it opened. Once inside, they started to explore. Jesse jumped on a wooden plank, and suddenly the floor gave way; a hole swallowed him in an instant.

His cousins raced over to the spot, but all they could hear was rushing water. They ran back to their parents in the park and yelled, "Jesse fell in a hole!"

The family soon discovered that Jesse had dropped twenty-five feet into a sewer pipe filled with water, untreated sewage, and toxic gas.

They immediately called 911, and soon, more than a hundred firefighters and rescue workers were trying to calculate where Jesse had gone to try to save him. The workers began opening manhole covers but the problem wasn't straightforward; the Los Angeles sewer system is a jumbled maze of underground pipes that follows the Los Angeles river and crosses underneath entire freeways.[7] They didn't know which pipe Jesse had gone into.

They searched for hours. It was now the middle of the night. The sanitation workers deployed remote cameras strapped onto flotation devices into different tunnels, looking for any sign of Jesse.

After almost twelve hours, when hope for the boy's survival in that toxic environment was waning, someone thought they saw handprints on the side of a pipe. Firefighters shut down the 134 freeway, and sanitation workers opened a maintenance shaft. Jesse had managed to find one of the few places in the labyrinth of pipes where there was a pocket of breathable air. He had wedged himself into it while sewage and water cascaded over him, and he'd prayed they would find him.[8]

When they opened the manhole and shone a light, there was Jesse, eleven feet down, looking up. News helicopters and reporters spread the word to all in Los Angeles who had been gripped by the story. It had taken twelve hours of creative thinking and hundreds of community resources persevering through fearful odds, but Jesse was alive![9]

This problem was well beyond Jesse's family's ability to resolve on their own. After doing all in their power to help Jesse, they asked for help from the community, who had expertise and tools critical to the success. Some of those experts had maps of the sewer system; others knew how to open manholes and shut down busy freeways. Social workers waited with the family. Volunteers brought food to the rescue teams as they worked. EMTs stood by for twelve hours until they were needed to rinse the sewage out of Jesse's eyes and ears. Reporters followed their progress and explained the dangers to others. Crews boarded up the old maintenance building so no one else would get hurt. There was tremendous catharsis and relief in the community when Jesse was found and safe. The resources in Los Angeles were relatively well developed, but this case required creatively adapting and a commitment that went long past what conventional wisdom would expect.

The questions in this category work to uncover what other resources beyond the local recipients' will be needed and who in the community might be best equipped and willing to help. The options are broad—municipal governments, educational facilities, faith groups, service clubs, communications outlets, grants, volunteer networks, philanthropists, politicians, non-government organizations, youth clubs. Often, finding the right combination of actors working together—as in Jesse's case—will be the most powerful solution.

Michael Nyenhuis of UNICEF USA will tell you that no single activity or organization can solve a complex problem. There is no silver bullet.

> It's sometimes attractive to just want to focus on a particular issue in your local community. That's fine, as long as you're aware that that one thing has to be combined with a bunch of other things to be effective. You don't necessarily need to do all those other things, but you want to be aware enough to recognize that the service you are offering is connected to others who are doing the other parts of the puzzle. You want to think about the holistic nature of the network.
>
> My wife and I are supporters of a non-profit immigrant services center in our community. They provide job training, English as a second language, some legal services, but they don't provide things like

> housing, access to food and shelter, med-
> ical care. One of the reasons I really like
> this service organization is because they
> know their lane, they know what they can
> do, what they're good at, and they know
> that their services are not the whole pic-
> ture. They have developed partnerships
> with others.[10]

Communities that regularly work together to solve problems develop an identity, or a story they tell themselves and others about the kind of community they are. We are the kind of community that proactively solves issues as they arise. We are the kind of community that won't allow violence or conflict to tear apart our social fabric. Having experiences working together, solving problems, weaves community fibers together and keeps them strong when something really tough happens.

As the executive director of a Near Eastern university studies program in Jerusalem, Israel, Eran Hayet explained that his work community has developed a culture of personal caring separate from other ethnic or religious labels and is enduring through tremendous stress. The facility has a mix of workers from many backgrounds and thrives on the simple rule: Don't talk politics or religion at work. Eran, whose Israeli family has a secular, socialist background, described how he feels working with his Palestinian colleagues.

> The most meaningful experience to me is when I visit my coworkers at home. In most cases, unfortunately, it is to pay condolences because someone has died, but I cannot believe the way I am received in their homes. They are very kind and hospitable to me. I always tell them that after hours, I am not your boss, we are completely equal, and we must treat each other that way.
>
> One evening at the Hadassah Hospital, I met one of my colleagues who works in security. I had brought my father into the emergency department, and my colleague was with his father-in-law.
>
> We saw each other, and he immediately came over to me and asked, "What can I do for you? Do you need any help? Do you need me to do something for you?" And I thought, "We are here for exactly the same reasons. I am an Israeli with my father; you are a Palestinian with your father-in-law, and we are in the emergency room." He greeted me like family. He made me feel that he really cared for me and my father—our relationship was more than just from our employment.[11]

Eran's example is of a workplace full of varied and intense political, religious, and cultural differences that, over time, is able to tell a more interesting story about the kind of community they are.

Four: What Will You Do When the Need Comes Up Next Time?

Sustainability is a buzz word in humanitarian work, and rightly so. It essentially means that if an intervention gets put in place and the problem arises again, the community is stronger and has a deeper reservoir of skills, knowledge, and relationships to address the problem with less need for outside help. They are more independent and self-reliant than they were before. There are certain kinds of questions that project into the future and can identify how to make the activities more lasting over time—in one word, sustainable.

Super-Typhoon Yolanda/Haiyan swept across the Philippines near Tacloban on November 8, 2013, and destroyed or damaged more than 1.1 million homes. It was the deadliest typhoon on record to strike the country and left more than 6,200 people dead, 28,000 injured, and 3 million displaced.[12] Local and international organizations partnered with the Philippine government and municipalities to help in the aftermath with food, shelter, medicine, sanitation, and cleanup. The Philippine people showed amazing resiliency in very difficult circumstances. But four months, six months, twelve months after the disaster—when the news cycle has moved on to other emergencies, when aid concerts and well-wishes on social media have faded—what happens then? What skills and knowledge are being developed that will strengthen the communities for the inevitable typhoons that will come again?

One sustainable, long-term focus in a disaster is to help people get back to work. It can happen in many creative ways. In Tacloban, the Buddhist Tzu Chi organization sponsored a cash-for-work program that employed 31,000 people a day for two weeks to remove storm debris. The group made huge progress in a short amount of time, cleaning up so rebuilding could begin. But even more importantly, the quick infusion of cash those individuals earned helped supply badly needed funds to purchase critical items the families needed to recover.[13]

My own organization recognized that building trades would be in high demand for the future and sponsored vocational training combined with on-the-job experience. Individuals who had lost their homes in the typhoon and were interested in learning a carpentry, electrical, or plumbing trade applied for the program. The families of each trainee received materials and tools to build a new house. Each family began to rebuild their own home with the assistance of one of the contracted professional carpenters and three other "carpenter trainees." In the next phases, the family worked with the professional plumber or electrician and their apprentices. Once their home was built, a member of the family committed to assist nine other families as one of the trained apprentices in building other shelters. When all ten homes were completed and the individuals had demonstrated their skills to the professionals on-site, they received a certificate from a vocational training institute verifying they could competently perform basic construction skills. Those individuals were then able to compete for the many construction jobs available in Tacloban and elsewhere.

These types of activities go beyond temporary assistance and create skills and knowledge that stand ready to be used in the future.

In addition to the gained skills, I don't think it's stretching the concept too far to say that the ultra-long-term objective of whatever activity is selected should be building the interior of people—their character. I wrote in the first chapter that one of the steel beams undergirding all service is the rescuing of that which is finest deep down inside each individual—their dignity and individual worth—and giving it an opportunity to grow and flourish. If we focus simply on the infrastructure of food, sanitation, security, and shelter, we miss the heart of the matter. We need and want to become better human beings over time. Intensely personal experiences with service, tolerance, listening, defending others, choosing to start again, forgiveness—these acts nurture character.

Ezra Taft Benson served as the US secretary of agriculture during the Eisenhower administration and later became the president of The Church of Jesus Christ of Latter-day Saints. He said in 1985:

> "[God] works from the inside out. The world works from the outside in. The world would take people out of the slums. Christ takes the slums out of people, and then they take themselves out of the slums. The world would mold men by changing their environment. Christ changes men, who then change their environment. The world would shape human behavior, but Christ can change human nature."[14]

It's not valid or helpful to tell people in impoverished circumstances that hard work will build character and that they can pull themselves up by their bootstraps. But having the opportunity to use new resources, make choices, seek consensus, solve problems, and be accountable affords us those experiences that build people from the inside out. Stronger character may be the ultimate sustainability.

Five: Is It a Local Solution?

The last category of questions is focused on how the local community can replicate the solutions with their local tools and supplies. Just as you are most powerful where you live, interventions have the highest likelihood of success when everything needed can be accessed locally.

I learned this through more sad mistakes than I can count.

One of them was a beautiful water project in Kenya. We proudly determined that rather than employing a noisy generator that used gasoline to pump the water into the storage tank, we would install sustainable solar panels to provide the power. It was a sunny part of the country, and we congratulated ourselves on this efficient, earth-friendly solution. However, it wasn't two weeks into its operation when a violent hailstorm broke out all the solar panels. The head of the water committee called our project manager and asked what they needed to do to repair the panels only to learn that the parts had to be ordered from Germany and would take months to arrive. The community had been so excited to have fresh drinking water, but it had lasted only two weeks because it wasn't a solution that could be repaired and cared for locally.

Local problems have often devoured my best intentions. The world is chock-full of expensive equipment donated with much fanfare that is now missing a bolt or a converter or some consumable supply, and it sits rusting in the yard, never able to perform its lifesaving work.

Local solutions for local problems. I sing it to myself like a lullaby. As harsh a reality as it may be, it's the only way things last.

Below is a case study—an opportunity for you to formulate for yourself some of the questions discussed in this chapter. The first line states the principle, the next line contains some details from a fictional scenario, and below that are some prompts to help you start asking questions. You can make it as complex or as simple an exercise as you like, but there is always much to learn in the details.

Case Study

PRINCIPLE: Ask and listen

CASE STUDY

A church congregation supplied Christmas stockings, wrapped toys, and food baskets to a women's shelter on Christmas Eve. The church members felt a glow of Christmas giving as they watched the kids tear into the packages with excitement. But one member of the congregation caught sight of the faces of the mothers who stood in the back of the hall. They looked miserable and surprisingly unhappy. You arrange to meet with the women's shelter leadership council and some of the women after the new year.

RESPONSE

- What questions would discover more about how the women would like to be supported?
- What lessons could the kids inadvertently be learning from the Christmas scenario in the shelter?
- How might the same need be addressed differently the following year?

PRINCIPLE: What are you able to do yourself?

CASE STUDY

You were surprised to learn that the mothers felt like failures and charity cases because they couldn't provide Christmas for their own kids and had to rely on the kindness and decisions of strangers. The kids were happy but could be overheard talking about how they hoped the church people would give them more stuff next year. One woman told you frankly, "I didn't want your charity. I wanted a job to buy my kids a Christmas—even a small one—so they don't forget their mother loves them even if we're living in the shelter right now."

There were three mothers who were not Christian but did not want to stand out by celebrating a different holiday.

The group discusses the comments and feelings the mothers expressed. Their desires to provide for their own children are strong. One woman wishes there could be a small store stocked with the same items the church donated for the kids but from which the mothers could pick out and wrap the gifts themselves.

RESPONSE

- Hearing this, what other questions would you ask?
- What questions might draw out ways the women can contribute to these new suggestions?
- How would the non-Christian families like to participate? What holidays are most important in their traditions? How would the families like to celebrate?

PRINCIPLE: What help do you want from the community?

CASE STUDY

The next autumn, the women at the shelter set up and decorate a tent with shelving and tables in preparation for a Celebration Store to open. It is stocked with donations from the church and community and a fair number of items made by the women at the shelter. The women have determined to open it from September through January to accommodate holidays from many cultures. It is staffed each Tuesday and Thursday evening by pairs of volunteers and mothers who consult with customers, wrap gifts, and talk with one another. The store becomes an informal gathering place. Some of the volunteers are women who lived at the shelter last year but have graduated from the program.

RESPONSE

- The success you are experiencing feels heady, but you worry that it is very dependent on volunteers from the church congregation. What will happen if they burn out or aren't able to volunteer every year? What could mitigate that potential challenge?

PRINCIPLE: What will happen when the problem arises next time?

CASE STUDY

One of the mothers told a volunteer that she wished she had a sewing machine. She used to make clothes for her kids. It sparks a discussion with the shelter leadership about potential classes to teach skills for employment beyond simple homemade Christmas gifts.

Two of the mothers and a member of the shelter staff meet with the local technical college. After weeks of meetings, the college agrees to open eight scholarships at their nearby campus for women from the shelter. The community volunteers offer to provide childcare.

RESPONSE

- Are there other underlying root issues that may need to be addressed? How would you ask about them?
- What unforeseen complications could derail this very welcome development from the technical college? How can the group look ahead?

PRINCIPLE: Is it a local solution that can be replicated by local people?

CASE STUDY

Over five years, a significant percentage of women entering the shelter leave with a marketable skill and certificate.

Many faith communities sign up to help with the Celebration Store. There is a tradition of graduates returning with their children to volunteer.

RESPONSE

- Which parts of this experience translate to other service organizations in the community and which do not?

CHAPTER 5

Protecting Dignity

5

Dignity

The five categories of questions in chapter 4 hopefully lead to relationships that are full of dignity and progress. It isn't possible to credibly help another person if the help begins on the premise that "I am rich, educated, and powerful so I will help you because you are poor, disadvantaged, and don't know much." This paternalistic worldview that infuses so much aid is predisposed to view people as victims from the outset.

I feel it is important to carefully acknowledge that true help is an exchange; it might not be an even exchange, but everyone benefits. However you determine to help another person, it's critical to recognize that the relationship is equal even if the circumstances may not be. Dignity is always possible, even without dignified conditions, but it requires eyes unblinded to see it.

Participation is an important key in protecting and sustaining the dignity of the people we are working alongside. People critically need to participate in their own development so that they *act* and are not just *acted upon*. Dignity and agency can be easily undermined by overlooking the thoughts, feelings, aspirations, and capabilities of people with needs.[1]

The stories that follow are examples of individuals putting concrete practices and policies into place that help people *feel* (or in some cases *not feel*) their inherent dignity and worth.

"They Have Nothing"

I once visited with a retired woman who had served as a church volunteer in India. She said that when she and her husband first arrived, they were overwhelmed by the heat, density, and noise. It was vastly different from the small town where they raised their children. The smells particularly were overpowering, and she had to force herself not to physically react to the strong odors they encountered. The couple was sad to see the many families who lived crowded together in small living quarters without much privacy.

She remembered writing to her family and friends, trying to convey the poverty she felt she was witnessing. "The people are so thin. They have absolutely nothing."

One Sunday, after they had been in the country about three months, a woman she had befriended at church took her aside and whispered confidentially to her, "We feel so sorry for you. What can we do to help you?"

The volunteer was taken aback. "You feel sorry for me? Why?"

"Well, you wear those terribly restricting clothes in the heat, and you seem so miserable. I saw the photo you showed of your home, and it looked so empty without your parents or your children to live with you. That must be very lonely for you. Come cook with us tomorrow, and let us be your Indian family. My mother and I will teach you our recipes. Would you like to come?"

All the time she was feeling sorry for them, they were feeling sorry for her. When she wrote in her letters that "they had nothing," she was ignoring hundreds of qualities they possessed—including kindness, humor, friendship, dignity, traditions, and the fun she soon discovered in her neighbors.

This is part of what it means to recognize the dignity in each human being. You have the chance to let go of preconceived ideas of what is poor and what is rich and value their human qualities separate from any possessions or attainment. When you can feel genuine respect, even if—especially if—others are living differently or hold different opinions from you, you have discovered the enduring truth that "they have everything."

We Dine Together

Denis Estimon moved to Boca Raton, Florida, as a Haitian immigrant when he was six years old. By the time he was attending Boca High School, he had learned the language and integrated into a large friend group, but he always remembered how lonely he felt during some of his years at school.

Denis told *CBS News*: "It's not a good feeling—like, you're by yourself, and that's something I don't want anybody to go through."[2]

So Denis started a club at school that he called We Dine Together. Students who belonged to the club spent their lunch period walking around the school, talking to anyone who was eating alone. In just one lunch period, they introduced themselves to dozens of students who were new to the school and some who were shy or socially insular.

Think back on your own experiences in a stratified school lunchroom. Some of my own were excruciating. And think now about what it would mean if one of the more popular kids in the school had said hello and sat by you for a while.

Denis graduated from Boca High and went on to partner with the Be Strong organization to open We Dine Together (www.wedinetogether.org) chapters to many other schools around the world. I appreciate that the idea takes less than forty-five minutes a day, costs no money, yet has the potential for huge gains in social capital among shyer or more hesitant students.

Watch the *CBS Sunday Morning* follow-up story about Denis Estimon here:

https://shdwmtn.com/cbs

A Holiday Bonus

I heard a story once that I can no longer document, but it remains a good example of how not to help.

A son said that his father worked at a car dealership. During the holidays, instead of giving out traditional bonuses, the owner of the dealership threw a big party for all the employees. At the height of the party, he would stand at the top of a staircase and fling cash bills into the crowd. There would be a mad scramble on the floor as everyone tried to grab the money. The boy remembers his father standing silently to the side while the melee was going on, refusing to join the free-for-all. The son related how proud he was that his father valued his own dignity more than the money, and he never forgot it.

The story stayed with me as well. There are so many instances when I see attempts to help other people as the equivalent of flinging cash at them and watching them scramble. I don't ever want to be in a position to demean the people I am hoping to serve.

Let Me Tell You My Story

Trisha Leimer was my neighbor for a while, but she most often lived in Frankfurt, Germany. Between 2016 and 2018, when Germany was especially focused on settling asylum seekers and refugees, Trisha and a dedicated corps of empathetic friends established hubs in Germany, Italy, and Greece to assist refugees. The group organized language and assimilation classes, assisted with legal matters, and worked to help people process their trauma. But one of the most interesting things Trisha did was collect experiences and publish the book *Let Me Tell You My Story*, in which the individuals told their histories in their own words. Photographs and original art, sometimes staged carefully to protect identities, accompany the vignettes in the book. The stories are harrowing to read, almost unimaginable in their details. I studied each photograph, looking for traces of all they had been through.

Sanaz from Syria shared one of the stories. She describes in matter-of-fact language her experiences that must have been unbearably intense.

> Our life was very good. We were very comfortable and happy. One day we went to sleep and awoke to find the planes bombing above us. The war had begun where we were. The bombs demolished our house and my uncle's house. My uncle died in the attack. So we left for Turkey.
>
> In Turkey my husband began working, but they didn't pay him for his work. We began to go hungry. My husband left before I did because we didn't have the money to leave with him. After a while my children and I left, and I also brought my husband's younger brother with me. I was five months pregnant. I suffered a lot on the way.
>
> We came by sea, and the smugglers abandoned us on a deserted island. We took off our life jackets and set them on fire to get warm. My children suffered with me. They were exhausted. They even got sick in their chests from the cold winds. We begged passing fishermen to rescue us. When we paid them money, they took us off the island.

I gave birth in a refugee camp and remained there for two months. I kept asking that they bring me, my husband, and my children back together. For months they told me, "You need to wait in court." In the end they sent me to a house where many other women and their children lived. I have one room for me and my family.

My husband and I are in the same country but in different cities. . . . We came from being under attack, and we still feel alienated here. We hope that after all this, our family will be back together for the sake of all these children.[3]

A radio interviewer asked Trisha a pointed question, noting that many of the people she interviewed had dire and precarious personal situations. They need basic necessities and safety; they are separated from family members and are looking for a place to call home. "You go in . . . and you take their picture, and you write down their details. . . . Exactly, what help is that?"[4]

Trisha's reply gets at the heart of the principle of protecting dignity and choice. She said:

One of the words that came up time after time when I was working with my friends was the word *dignity*. The individuals I interviewed had lost everything material in their lives. And yet they were some of the most grateful people I knew because they had figured out what it was that really mattered.

Even so, losing dignity and standing was perhaps their greatest loss. They were coming into a country that was often fearful of them, and fear can do a lot of weird things to people. Having the chance to tell their story, portraying themselves not as a refugee but as a mother or a father, as a teacher or a lab assistant or a truck driver—that helped them be seen as equals. There is great dignity in being seen as an equal.

And there is dignity in having somebody listen to your story and care. When we were recording the stories, they were so grateful that somebody actually wanted to take the time to listen to what happened to them. They didn't tell their stories to each other in the camps because everybody else had trauma too—everyone else was having a hard time and just trying to keep their head above water. Time after time, they would stand up from speaking, take a deep breath, and say, "Thank you." It was for nothing more than just listening. It was the dignity of being listened to.

We also gave them choices about the stories themselves. We asked them, "How would you like us to tell your story? Would you prefer to use your name or a different name? Would you like to be anonymous? Would you prefer to be photo-graphed or not?" Preserving those choices is very important in a very undignified situation.[5]

For me, the book was a work of brilliance. At its most basic, *Let Me Tell You My Story* insists that every individual is a unique treasure with a story worth remembering and a life worthy of safe passage and reverence. The stories provoke in me—even a handful of years after they were recorded—a particular admiration and connection. I feel as though I have met the individuals myself. I can't help but send up a prayer that each of them is now writing more peaceful chapters in their ongoing life stories.

Six Months of Dignified Walking

A seventeen-year-old boy in Norway submitted a story from St. Hallvard Upper Secondary School to commemorate Global Dignity Day. He wrote:

> "My story about dignity is about a good friend of mine. He has a younger brother who has an illness that makes him very nervous about new things. His younger brother was supposed to start eighth grade and he was, as I said, very nervous. My friend decided to walk his brother to school for as long as it took for him to feel that he could

go on his own. He walked him to school for six months."[6]

Greyston Bakery's Open Hiring

Greyston Bakery was founded in Yonkers, New York, by Bernie Glassman, a practicing Zen Buddhist. Its mission is to make and sell 35,000 pounds of brownies a day, but it has a unique hiring practice. People put their name on a list, and when a slot opens, the bakery calls the next name on the list. No matter their background or lack of qualifications, they get a job. For Dion, who had just been released from serving four years in prison for selling drugs, it was the second chance he desperately wanted. Upworthy News shared his story.[7]

> "I had a whole lot of time to think and re-flect on life. I knew life wasn't about being in a cell. It was just time to change my ways. I came home with nothing, not a dime. I was looking for employment, nobody would hire me. . . . Then a friend reminded me about Greyston. . . . I put my name on the list for a job. One day . . . I got a call [asking if I would] come to work. And I came alive. My first day at work I was excited. I [saw] people I knew, and they [were] encouraging me because we've all been through the same things. . . . I went from apprentice to lead operator to research and

development. Now recently, I just got promoted to supervisor training. I never thought that the bakery could do this for me. I started my own family, I have my first child.

"I'm not rich, no, but I'm happy. . . . Everybody deserves a second chance. You've got to get to know people. When you give a person a job, you're giving that person a second chance at life."

Greyston Bakery donates all profits to its parent company, the Greyston Foundation, and is widely acknowledged for its innovative hiring practices that offer people a chance for a dignified new start.

Watch Dion's entire story here:
https://shdwmtn.com /greystonbakery

ANN POWER-FORDE
HUMAN RIGHTS JURIST

Dignity is not a right; it is a reality from which rights are derived. Just as natural families have a shared genetic makeup, the human family carries a "shared imprint of value." To respect the dignity of another is to recognize the "family resemblance." However undignified our actions or degrading our circumstances, we are born with dignity, we live with dignity, and we die with dignity.[8]

NELSON MANDELA

Overcoming poverty is not a gesture of charity. It is an act of justice. It is the protection of a fundamental human right, the right to dignity and a decent life.[9]

PATRICK PARKINSON
DEAN OF LAW, TC BEIRNE SCHOOL OF LAW, UNIVERSITY OF QUEENSLAND, AUSTRALIA

Children are not born with much dignity—either for the mother or the child. They are delivered through pain and anguish, come forth into the world covered in human fluids, and must first be washed before being presented to relatives. Their first sounds are those of distress. Yet in every newborn we recognize an inherent dignity, because God has created them as unique and precious individuals. By respecting their dignity, in all their helplessness, we honor the inherent worth of all humanity. Babies act as a mirror to us to realize that for all our faults, we too have inherent and incomparable worth.[10]

ELEANOR ROOSEVELT

[Universal human rights begin] in small places, close to home—so close and so small that they cannot be seen on any maps of the world . . . . Such are the places where every man, woman, and child seeks equal justice, equal opportunity, equal dignity without discrimination. Unless these rights have meaning there, they have little meaning anywhere.[11]

GANOUNE DIOP
SECRETARY GENERAL, INTERNATIONAL RELIGIOUS LIBERTY ASSOCIATION

The deepest truth about human dignity is the belief that human beings are sacred, more important than holy sites or sacred places. Humans are temples of the divine, holy habitations worthy of respect.[12]

Questions to Consider

- What stories do you know that demonstrate dignity even in undignified conditions?

- What equivalents have you seen of flinging money at people and watching them scramble?

- How has someone else protected your own dignity and self-respect? How did they do it?

- What words do you use to describe the reasons human dignity is important in your own life and work?

Attacking Root Causes and Nurturing Long-Term Solutions

6

_____

Agnes had two sons and no food. The Great Depression was raging, and she was a young widow. She was in trouble, every day trying to scrape together enough food for the three of them to eat. Her dream of homesteading a wheat farm in Montana with her husband had disintegrated when Ebert died of scarlet fever. She'd had to sell the store and house in town and move to California to ride out the bad times, but she wouldn't sell the farm. It was the boys' inheritance—the only thing their father could do for them now.

Bill, her eldest, was twelve years old. The only money coming into the household was from his daily paper route. One of his deliveries was to a bakery, and they paid in donuts every morning. She was grateful, but she worried about nutrition for the growing boys. Agnes made the rounds to the agencies to apply for assistance, but when they found out she still owned the farm in Montana, she was disqualified. "Many other families are hungry and don't have land to sell," they said.

One morning, Bill came into the house carrying a case of canned milk. An entire beautiful case—precious cans that they could open at their leisure without it spoiling. "It was on the porch," Bill told her with some wonderment in his eyes. The box had a tag saying it was from the Salvation Army. They had received Agnes's request and had responded without any conditions to her hungry family.

Agnes was my great-grandmother. Bill was my grandfather. This story has been handed down through the generations in my family. Whenever my mother told it to me, she would hand me a twenty-dollar bill and direct me to greet the Salvation Army bell ringer and tuck the money inside the red kettle.

"Don't ever forget," she would say, "that the Salvation Army helped our family when no one else would." Even now, every Christmas, my far-flung family members and I still put bills into kettles placed outside hardware stores and grocery centers, remembering.

I met Commissioners Ken and Jolene Hodder of the Salvation Army in 2021 when Ken became the National Commander for the United States and Jolene was appointed the National Secretary for the program. Becoming exposed to the breadth of their organizations, I came to understand that their mission goes much deeper than the emergency food that blessed my family.

The Salvation Army was founded in London in 1865 by William and Catherine Booth. Their purpose was to help individuals in poverty find ways to address both their physical and spiritual needs. The Salvation Army today is an evangelical part of the universal Christian church and functions in 134 countries around the globe. It operates hospitals, schools, homes for the aged, youth programs, mitigation for the unhoused, addiction recovery groups, and many other activities targeting the root causes of poverty. The mission is the same today as it has always been: "To preach the gospel of Jesus Christ and to meet human needs in His name without discrimination."[1]

Organisation for Economic Co-operation and Development (OECD) data from 2019 shows that nearly 21 percent of the children in the United States live in poverty. The United States has the highest child-poverty rate among the world's wealthiest twenty-six nations. Children who live in poverty are much more likely to remain in poverty as adults. The epidemic of inter-generational poverty, passed down from one generation to the next, is not only the result of a lack of resources but also a shortage of life skills and an absence of people to trust.[2]

The Salvation Army launched Pathway of Hope in 2011. For the organization, it was a pivotal shift to focusing on the root causes of poverty. Rather than simply treating the symptoms, they reorganized their programming to support long-term solutions. Pathway of Hope offers targeted services for families who want to break the cycles of poverty and find a path out of constant crisis.

First, each family commits to the process and makes a personal plan. What do they want to do in the next six months? What help do they need to get there? They are then assigned a dedicated case manager who helps them connect to resources, encourages them, and tracks their progress as they master a series of life skills. The Salvation Army deploys its internal resources to offer the clients job training, healthcare services, childcare, school enrollment, affordable housing options, and legal services. When it works at its best, families progress from crisis to stability and eventually self-sufficiency with the ability to help others.[3]

Since its beginning, the Pathway of Hope program has served more than 19,000 families across the United States, impacting 20,000 adults and more than 38,000 children, 80 percent of whom are under the age of twelve. Beyond the immediate results of job counseling, food and utility assistance, budget planning, and the other services wrapped up in Pathway of Hope, there is a discernible long-term impact on the next generation. In fact, more than 75 percent of the adults interviewed felt more hopeful about their children's future than they did before they enrolled.

Commissioner Hodder described how satisfying it is to celebrate the many different physical milestones with these families but that for him, seeing the hope born in the process may be the most rewarding outcome of all.

> "Whenever someone begins to hope, when they sense that their circumstances can improve, and when they find people in whom they can put their trust—it is like a booster rocket gets lit inside them. It changes everything. And beyond the impact on their own life, it has an enormous influence on their children and their opportunities."[4]

Ken tells a story that reveals this arc of hope and the deep longing for renewal and a new start that lies dormant in so many people's hearts.

> A few years ago, I visited one of the Salvation Army's adult rehabilitation centers, which is where individuals suffering from a range of issues, including substance abuse, will come for help. I happened to be there on graduation night. The hall was filled with men and women in the program, all grappling with problems that had caused them to lose their homes, their livelihoods, and their families.

During the course of the evening, a side door opened, and the graduates, dressed in gowns and mortar boards, came to the center of the platform. They started to sing a series of songs that were punctuated by individuals briefly telling their own stories of recovery. It was marvelous to watch.

It all came to a head, however, when one man took the microphone and said, "I thank God and the Salvation Army for giving me my family back." He dropped the mic and walked out in front of the choir, where he knelt facing the congregation and opened his arms wide. All eyes went instantly to the back of the room, where we saw a small girl of about seven or eight years of age with long brown hair.

When that little girl saw her father kneeling in front of her, she started to run down the aisle toward him. And as she did so, time seemed to slow down. I looked at the congregation, and I thought to myself that everyone watching that little girl was watching as a portion of their own life, lost for whatever reason, was miraculously restored to them. The men cheered, and the women wept. And when the girl finally reached her father and leaped into his arms, he lifted her and gave her a big kiss on the cheek. The place went wild.

> That moment probably best symbolizes the restoration, redemption, reconciliation, and love that the Salvation Army hopes to see in every life, in everyone who comes to us. And it's the kind of thing that keeps me going.[5]

The Salvation Army asked itself hard questions about how its programs could better understand root causes and then organized to create longer-term solutions. In a similar way, I've found I need to ask a lot of questions and then question the assumptions underlying the answers before I can understand root causes. Why is it like this? How did we get here? What would make it permanently different? For example, a lot of energy goes into collecting food for food pantries, but why do people in our community need so much emergency food? Who are the big users of food pantries? What is creating the resource gaps in their lives? Is anyone successfully addressing those gaps that drive the need for the emergency food? What would need to be different so that families wouldn't need to use the food pantry as often? Can I contribute something to that root solution?

I never forget that the answer is going to include more than just money. Root problems almost always boil down to relationships or the lack of them among groups. Creating positive relationships in new forms can be the lifeblood of a root solution.

I saw this when I visited a CARE International project in Ethiopia. The heart of the project was a village savings-and-loan association. Approximately twenty-five interested people gathered and formed a group. It was usually made up of neighbors and friends who lived close, because they had to commit to meeting in person once a week. They agreed to some formal rules and elected a chair, vice chair, and treasurer. They bought three keys for their lockbox where the savings were kept, and all three officers had to be present whenever it was opened.

Every member agreed to save a minimum of twenty-five cents a week, but they could save more if they had it. At the end of three months of weekly savings, there would be at least $75 in the savings account.

Now members of the group can use that capital to apply for small loans at an interest rate set by the group—usually 3–5 percent. The group can only fund a few projects at a time, but it depends on the size of the loans. Together, they select the most viable proposals. The group still meets every week to make their savings-and-loan payments to their peers. At the end of another three months, the first cycle of loans has been repaid, and the interest has been shared out to the group. Then they launch another cycle.

During the weekly meetings, members are also getting technical training on animal husbandry, irrigation gardening, home improvements, and other topics in which they have interest. At the end of twelve months, the formal agreement ends. However, 90 percent of the groups keep going and regulate themselves without any outside help. As the groups develop over time, their savings allow them to do bigger, collective projects. Some of the older groups I visited were leasing land for farming, putting up storage sheds, or buying cooperative milling equipment. The discipline of saving each week certainly provided the capital for each member to make improvements, but I was struck by how much trust and social cohesion developed in the savings-and-loan groups among people who lived close geographically but were very different in other ways. There is a tremendous positive societal wealth in this kind of relationship building.

The Tadesse family joined a savings group seven years ago. Before that, Mr. Tadesse told me that they lived every day looking for what they would eat. If any emergency happened, they had to borrow money from the village lenders, who charged 100 percent interest. If you borrow 100, you pay back 200. The Tadesses have five children. The family had food in the rainy season but not in the dry season. They lived in a traditional round hut with a thatched roof.

They used their first loan to buy six chickens. They had received technical training from CARE on how to build a coop and give the necessary poultry vaccinations. They

had a voucher for chicken wire, but they purchased every-thing else themselves.

The chickens began laying eggs. At first, the family wanted to sell the eggs, but they learned in their classes how important it was for children and pregnant women to eat protein every day. Mrs. Tadesse was pregnant, so they began cooking with the eggs. They gathered thirty eggs each week, and they would eat fifteen and sell fifteen.

They used their next loan to buy a goat and some fattening feed. They fattened the goat and sold it during the Easter/Passover season when everyone eats meat for the holiday.

Then they began keeping bees that like the flowering Blue Gum Eucalyptus trees around their property. The family sells the honey and the comb at certain times of

the year and then "waters" the bees with a mixture of oil, water, and flour during the dry season. I counted fourteen hives on their property.

They used the income from the bees to dig a hand-pumped well in their yard. They had to dig eighteen meters down to hit water, and it was not potable, but it was good for irrigation.

With water on their property, they planted fruit trees—avocado, mango, banana—and figured out an easy drip irrigation system for a vegetable garden. They ate the fruits and vegetables and sold produce in the market.

Next, they built a new house with a modern metal roof and painted it a bright coral color. They moved out of their

round thatched hut and turned it into a stable for the cow they bought. They can fatten one to two cows every season for sale and get a very good price.

Their two oldest children took the entrance exams and scored high enough to be accepted into university. The day I visited, there was a congratulations banner tacked above the front door because the oldest boy had just graduated from teacher's college and the oldest girl from pharmacy

school. When I asked what the family's next project was going to be, they said they knew life was still unsettled, they didn't want to "backslide," but their goal was to maintain all they had learned, keep saving to send their younger three to school, and not depend on anyone else for their living ever again.

I came away energized by how extremely small savings over time can make a big difference in the options a family has. Additionally, the relationships in the peer group helped them develop discipline and expertise to solve the problems that inevitably arise.

Even though the Tadesse family are still concerned that they will face additional hurdles, they successfully interrupted the poverty cycle for their children. They went from having uncertain sources for food every day and eating very poorly in the dry season to seeing their oldest children

graduate from university with professional degrees. And they accomplished it by saving twenty-five cents a week.

But it wasn't only saving the twenty-five cents that made the difference. The family chose to participate and made their own decisions about how to utilize the savings and loans. Additionally, the social relationships of trust developed within the savings group and the expertise the members could draw upon from CARE were huge factors in their success.

This progress toward self-reliance was taking place in a rural part of Ethiopia, but I wondered if the same core elements would produce successful outcomes in a context like the United States, even if the problem were a different one.

I wrote earlier that the United States has the highest child-poverty rate among the world's wealthiest twenty-six nations. It also has surprisingly high infant and maternal mortality rates. The poverty and mortality rates for Black mothers are more than double what they are for other mothers. The reasons for this inequity are complex.[6]

These statistics were on the mind of Vickie Terry, the executive director of the Memphis Branch of the NAACP, when she met with community faith leaders in Memphis, Tennessee.

> "It disturbs me that [we] are sitting in a zip-code that has one of the highest infant mortality rates in the country."[7]

The community wanted to help Vickie change that statistic. They called on the experience of Dr. Michael V. Beheshti—a humanitarian service coordinator and a practicing physician. Dr. Beheshti began looking through medical literature and found surprisingly little that was helpful on the topic until he stumbled across a peer-reviewed paper from The Ohio State University Wexner Medical Center. It described a community-based program that focused on certain determining factors that contributed to poor infant and maternal outcomes in Black populations.

The Ohio program, founded by Dr. Patricia Gabbe, proposed that (similar to the Salvation Army interventions) it was food insecurity, unstable housing, unreliable transportation, the lack of available childcare, and other basic necessities that were increasing the risk factors for mothers and infants in ways not always apparent to the medical establishment. Over several years, the Ohio State interventions had brought the infant mortality rate in Weinland Park, Ohio, (a Columbus neighborhood) from 15/1,000 births to 3/1,000 births. The average in the United States is 5.6/1,000 births.

Vickie Terry and Dr. Beheshti wanted to replicate those outcomes in Memphis. They recognized right away that trusted community volunteers would play a critical role in connecting parents with health, nutrition, education resources, and government services. Community volunteers could also create a network for transportation, food, and housing resources. In 2022, the MyBaby4Me initiative began in Memphis, Tennessee. The program accepts women at any stage of pregnancy and continues with her through the first year of her baby's life.

Dr. Gabbe and the OSU medical team offered all their documentation and lessons learned to the Memphis partnership. A volunteer couple in the community—a retired pharmacist and a nurse—headed up the volunteer outreach and organized more than 1,000 rides for new or expectant mothers so they could make their doctors' appointments.

The NAACP hosted weekly maternal classes in their offices, taught by volunteers and experienced parents.

The results in the twelve months of operation were impressive. In the first fifteen months, MyBaby4Me Memphis served over thirty unique high-risk mothers through 118 formal gatherings. It provided over 1,000 individual contacts with mothers and their children, 700 meals, 600 bags of groceries, and more than 500 gift cards to women for gasoline or other necessities. Additionally, those mothers from a very high-risk population safely delivered their healthy babies.

Ashley Martin was the mother of one of those babies. She was eight weeks pregnant with her first child, completely scared, and hadn't told anyone she was expecting. She didn't know what to do. She saw a TV ad describing MyBaby4Me, so she called the number. One of the community volunteers answered and calmly assured her, "Don't worry, it's going to be okay." The volunteer invited Ashley to come to an upcoming mothers' class.

Ashley came every week for the duration of her pregnancy and learned information about nutrition during pregnancy, car seat safety, safe sleeping with infants, and much more. Now Ashley encourages other expectant mothers in her neighborhood to attend the classes and get the support.

Ashley said, "I'm better prepared. I understand what it means to take care of your child in the first couple of weeks. . . . Every time I come [to class], I learn something new."[8]

Because of the success, similar MyBaby4Me partnerships have begun in other cities.[9]

The Salvation Army, CARE, and MyBaby4Me showcase how seemingly intractable problems were addressed by building community support systems that led to self-reliance, but not every effort succeeds. I often wonder why it is so difficult for us as human beings to change our behaviors when the behaviors aren't productive. The Tadesse family was able to use the village savings model to transform their family life, but what about the many others whose stories do not end so cleanly or as positively? What about those who do not seem to have the personality or confidence to even try the Salvation Army's Pathway of Hope? I don't know the answer to these questions. I do know I am poor at predicting who will or will not leverage the resources in a way that works, so I keep offering resources. I remember that God loves the unlikely, and there is a lot of unlikely success in this world.

My great-grandmother Agnes intuitively knew not to sell the land. It was her family's best chance to be independent from aid, the foundation of the self-reliance she could offer her sons. The farm eventually went to Bill and was then passed down to my mother, Jean. My siblings and I worked in the late summers during the harvest. We rode in the combines and took truckloads of grain to the scales in town. We listened carefully to how much protein each section produced and followed the price per bushel. The profit from the sale of the wheat every year helped pay for our school tuition and weddings. The wheat farm was part of sustaining my family for nearly 100 years.

The Salvation Army was savvy enough to pivot to a hope-filled, long-term path that lets families practice the skills and resources they need to leave poverty permanently behind. The Tadesse family learned to patiently plan for incremental progress and structure their self-reliance to withstand inevitable shocks. The Memphis community demonstrated that different segments of society who have not traditionally interacted with each other can face down their preconceived ideas, bring new understanding and energy to an old problem, and literally save lives.

I share the stories in this chapter because it can be shockingly easy to spend all our charitable energy on the symptoms of poverty and never attack the root causes. Even worse, our emergency assistance, not paired with longer-term solutions, can add to dependency and make a situation worse over time. Attacking root causes and nurturing long-term solutions are what lead to real impact over time.

Questions to Consider

- Are there other principles you think belong in this discussion?

- What are some of the root causes of the issues that concern you?

- Who is doing work you admire? What do you want to do yourself? How will you start?

Volunteerism— The Social Movement

7

President George H. W. Bush once remarked that "the solution to each problem that confronts us begins with an individual who steps forward and who says: I can help."[1]

Definitions of Volunteerism

A 2018 report found that almost 80 million Americans volunteer and give nearly 6.9 billion hours of their time, worth an estimated $167 billion in economic value.[2] Teenage and midlife adult volunteering rates more than doubled over the last few decades.[3] Millions of others informally volunteer by supporting family, friends, and neighbors. But why do they do it?

Volunteerism can be defined as "offering unpaid labor or expertise in the service of improving communities or to support nonprofit organizations." Volunteers work to advance the lives of community members out of a desire to give back, feelings of social responsibility, or an active expression of love of God and others. Volunteering is a special activity because it cuts both ways—it meets needs in both givers and receivers. It oils the squeaks in communities willing to carry each other's burdens and share each other's joys.

Organized Volunteerism

Organized volunteerism in the United States can be traced back to the Revolutionary War, when civilians smelted ammunition and fed and clothed the Continental army. More formal volunteering around the world began in the 1800s with organizations such as the YMCA, started by George Williams in London in 1844, and the American Red Cross, founded by Clara Barton in 1881.

The twentieth century saw a sharp rise in the establishment of voluntary organizations and service clubs dedicated to making positive local impact. Rotary International is one of the largest and most well-known service clubs in the world. Begun in 1905 as the Rotary Club of Chicago by attorney Paul Harris, it was simply Paul and three friends with varied professional experiences (an engineer, a coal merchant, and a tailor) whom he invited to exchange ideas and form meaningful relationships. It was named the Rotary Club because they originally rotated their meeting place among each other's establishments of business. Its purpose was for professionals with different backgrounds, cultures, and beliefs to exchange ideas, form lifelong friendships, and serve together.[4] Over time, Rotary began to address various humanitarian challenges around the world. Today, there are more than 45,000 Rotary Clubs in more than 200 countries. One of the Rotarians' two official mottos is Service Above Self.[5]

John Hewko is the current General Secretary and CEO of Rotary International. John spoke movingly in Melbourne, Australia, about the ways voluntary service can tackle toxic polarization and contribute to peace.

> Building peace is more than just ending war. It's also about taking on the challenges of food insecurity, the climate crisis, civil unrest, and toxic polarization. These are huge challenges. But this is not a moment for despair. Rather, this is [our] moment to step up and take action. Because this is what we do. We are practitioners of peace, and this gives us an opportunity to fulfill our historic role—one that has been built through our decades-long investments in peace. Because today, peace is an imperative. And that imperative begins with us because we have the means to wage peace as aggressively as nations can wage war.[6]

I resonate with the image of waging peace as aggressively as nations wage war. It's easy to think of volunteering as a one-time commitment or an occasional activity—perhaps we reserve it for after we retire when we have more time to get involved in "causes"—but John and others see that volunteering can essentially become an outlook, a way of life.

Volunteering for Peace

In a world that is gradually growing more isolated and more polarized, volunteerism is a mindset that says "I am willing to do something for the good of the whole." It's a way of constructively turning down social stress and political heat. It promotes peace by experiencing peace. It's difficult to be angry with someone you serve or serve with. Or as Utah Governor Spencer Cox is fond of saying, "It's hard to hate someone up close."[7]

In my worldview, volunteerism is a radical independence from any attempt to monetize caring. I feel strong personal desires to preserve social actions that have nothing to do with profit or politics.

Barron Segar is the CEO of the World Food Programme USA and is a passionate defender of neutrality. He told me about a dramatic exchange that occurred as he spoke to volunteers and donors, and it reminds me that we don't ever truly possess the tools for judging each other's potential or future.

I was attending an event where we were honoring somebody for their philanthropy. I was talking about the need to help people globally who are suffering, and a gentleman at one of the tables clinked on his glass. I thought he was going to give a toast. Instead, he said, "I have a question for you. Why are we helping the future terrorists of the world?"

I stopped and thought, "Okay, how am I going to respond to this?" I took a deep breath and said, "First, thank you for asking the question. I don't know about you, but I don't have the power to know who will fall into extremism and who will not, to decide who lives and who dies. I have a fundamental belief that people are good. I also have a fundamental belief that if young people have access to education and opportunity, they will be able to do their best and succeed.

"You mentioned funding the future terrorists of the world. I happen to believe that if people who are very vulnerable are given opportunities— access to food, education, and emotional care— they have the chance to do something truly great with their lives. My goal in speaking here tonight is to make sure that every single individual has an opportunity to make that kind of life with the trust that fewer people will fall into terrorism."[8]

Barron's story reveals that it is never helpful to think of "community" in the abstract and attach labels, as if every person in the community holds the same views. It's amazing to me to note that throughout history, adversity has tended to strengthen communities instead of eroding them.

Larry Keeley is an innovation scientist, writer, and passionate professor at IIT Institute of Design in Chicago. When I asked him how volunteerism might have the potential to promote peace, he responded with his characteristic boldness that the problems won't be solved by *them* but by *us*. He further said:

> Consider this: About half the country thinks *government is the enemy*. The other half thinks *government is the answer*. What if both sides are wrong? We have real, pressing, complicated problems in nearly every community. People struggle. Problems are real, often acute. Solutions are elusive.
>
> When community problems are viewed through our modern sense of *divisiveness*, half the people will *blame the government for negligence and gross incompetence*. The other half will

wonder, desperately, *When will someone, anyone, show up to fix this mess?* Both reactions share the same error: They see "the government" as something external, not as *us*.

Once you stop making this error, the answer becomes instantly clear: *Do something. Make the problem yours, not the government's. Help whoever needs help. You may not have the perfect answer, but that doesn't matter. You simply have to care and act. When you do, you will learn from the people most affected. You'll figure stuff out. Together. And guess what? Whoever is in trouble, they will love you for your effort. And you will learn to love yourself a little more, and see your own cares and troubles in a new light.*[9]

Larry's point that problems are mutually ours to work on—that showing up and caring are already solutions—leads to a logical next step. What tools can communities use to begin working together?

One of those tools to leverage is the public officials elected to serve. As we act on issues we care deeply about, we gain a growing awareness of nuanced positions and subtle inequities—aspects that could be better or fairer or more inclusive. Government is—or should be—about public service. If we want to address the root causes of social problems, uplift people in sustainable ways, and treat everyone with the dignity they inherently deserve, then public policy and legislation are some of the most important tools in the toolbox. We can participate in school board meetings and city councils, we can share our priorities with our elected officials, and we can even run for office ourselves.

Volunteering with JustServe

Many want to step forward to contribute to solutions in their communities, but they don't know exactly what to do or how to start. Organic opportunities have always been available through Lions Club, Rotary, Daughters of the American Revolution, and other service clubs. The sociality among the members is an important part of the draw. But what does "stepping forward to help" look like in the digital age? JustServe has an interesting way of answering that question.

JustServe is a social movement working to accelerate peace and understanding at the neighborhood level. It strengthens social fabric by promoting shared community projects and attracting volunteers from among its users. Active in seventeen countries and still expanding, it serves as a community of practice for volunteerism that is hopeful, thoughtful, and effective—like a service club without borders. Larry Keeley, Paul Cobb, and John Hewko are members of the JustServe advisory council and help promote the unique richness of volunteerism in society. JustServe is built on the premise that volunteer service is an extension of who we are, not specifically what we do.

The JustServe movement is supported by an app and website that act as a search engine to identify local volunteer opportunities by zip code. Tens of thousands of opportunities have been posted since 2012, and hundreds of thousands of volunteers have responded. JustServe is open to the public and—important to me—it is free. It's easy to find or post projects, and personal information is not utilized or sold.

Calling up JustServe.org in my home zip code as I write this chapter, I see that I can register to bring lunch to the homeless youth center, chat with refugee women who are improving their English online, help kids learn to use a climbing wall at a wetland center, read twice a week with students at an elementary school, teach a computer class to new community residents, or harvest tomatoes and vegetables at a community garden. Those are just a few of the listings in my own town over the next three days. JustServe is a concrete way communities can act to respond to problems.

Paul Cobb marched for civil rights as a young man with Dr. Martin Luther King Jr. He became a well-respected journalist, publisher, and civic leader based in Oakland,

California. Speaking about volunteer service to a group of civic leaders in 2019, he said,

> "If Martin Luther King were alive today, he would be a charter-member of JustServe. JustServe is a movement . . . that asks people all over the world to 'just serve' their fellowman and the fellow community members and to volunteer and to extend the hand! And that is the essence of belief put to work."[10]

President M. Russell Ballard, one of the presiding apostles in The Church of Jesus Christ of Latter-day Saints until he passed away in 2023, was an early promoter of JustServe. Having traveled the world and noted the needs, he said simply,

> "When we serve together, we realize that our similarities are stronger than our differences. [As people help and lift each other through JustServe and other service opportunities] the light of Jesus Christ is spread and increased throughout the world."[11]

Pamela's Rules for Volunteering

My work in Salt Lake City has crossed paths with Pamela Atkinson's many times. She is an Elder in the First

Presbyterian Church and an absolutely tireless advocate for homeless, refugee, and low-income families in my home state of Utah. She was raised by a single mother in a poverty pocket of London. She and her sisters routinely lined their shoes with cardboard to cover the holes, and she told me once that she didn't know about top sheets on a bed until she visited a friend. At age fourteen, she resolved to dedicate herself to school and make a life for herself through education. She became a registered nurse in the UK, worked in Australia, and finally made her home in the United States, where she became an adviser to four Utah governors and grew to be an iconic figure in humanitarian circles.

Pamela is an especially compassionate leader and treats all people, however they look or sound or smell, with careful dignity and respect. I have seen her gently put a hand on the shoulder of a man sleeping under a tree in the park. When he awoke, she asked him if he would like some water. Or would he come out of the sun? Did he want to come into the shelter, or would he like some toiletries? She could have been speaking to King Charles with all the deference and dignity she gave the man.

In an interview with *Forbes Magazine*, Pamela described the rules she has made for herself to be an effective volunteer and build on common ground:[12]

1. **Ego has no role in service**. Be content to be an ordinary person happily helping behind the scenes. It's not about you; it's about them.

2. **Collaboration**. *Coordinate*, *cooperate*, and *collaborate* are three Cs of service, but *collaborate* is the greatest. After Pamela launched her homeless outreach program in 1991, another agency wanted to run and expand the program. She was open to the collaboration and participated in their expanded program herself for more than twenty years.

3. **Don't "be afraid to speak out."** "If I feel strongly about an injustice, an issue that is not being addressed in a collaborative and focused way, I need to speak out," she says. She has learned with experience that even if a room full of people openly oppose her, there are others who show their support more privately and express their gratitude for her leadership.

4. **Never let issues interfere with relationships**. While lobbying Utah's legislators for support for her programs over the years, she's learned never to let disagreements interfere with relationships. "By not destroying relationships, I can go back again on other issues." She does this by truly listening to opposing points of view, often with the invitation, "I've never thought of it that way—tell me more."

5. **Treat volunteers with respect**. "Ask the volunteers, 'How are things going? Are you enjoying this?' Ask volunteers for ideas to improve service." Too many organizations fail to appreciate the value of their volunteers.

6. **Don't give up**. When she hears "no," she asks, "What can I do to help change your mind?" She offers to provide tours, introductions, whatever it will take to change a mind.

7. **Everyone can do something**. She was once challenged by a woman who said, "I'm eighty years old, I rarely get out of the house, and I have a limited income. How can I make a difference?" Pamela challenged her to donate a can of soup to the food bank each week. She took the challenge, and for several years thereafter, she did just that, ultimately providing hundreds of meals for people who otherwise might have gone hungry.

8. **Power of touch and a smile**. While volunteering with the Salvation Army years ago, Pamela was assigned by the major to greet each homeless person attending dinner that evening with a warm smile and a hearty handshake because some of the homeless hadn't been touched in the last week. She's never forgotten that lesson and makes a point to always greet people, especially the poor, with a smile and handshake or other appropriate touch.

9. **Avoid emotional bankruptcy**. You cannot take care of others unless you first take care of yourself. "Your

family and friends" support you, and you support them. It helps everyone carry on.

10. "**I can do all things through Christ who strengtheneth me**." Pamela sometimes feels inspired by a divine influence in her work and credits her faith in Jesus Christ for her strength. But she clearly recognizes that many of her non-churchgoing friends carry themselves and their responsibilities just as strongly and are among the kindest and most generous people she knows.

I asked earlier why so many individuals find satisfaction and value in volunteerism when it is surely inconvenient, people can be annoying, it takes precious time, and no one is getting paid.

Over the years, the word *charity* has lost its original shine. We talk about "charity cases" or "not accepting charity" with an arched eyebrow. But the Apostle Paul wrote that charity suffers long and is kind; it doesn't envy others or puff itself up. It doesn't seek for its own attention; it is not easily provoked. Charity doesn't rejoice in other people's troubles but rejoices in what is true. It bears all things, believes all things, hopes all things, endures all things (see 1 Corinthians 13:4–8). All things must pass away, but charity is the pure love of Christ, which endures forever (Moroni 7:47).

We volunteer in so many inconvenient settings and even hope to foster a social movement of volunteerism because it spins off friendships, enhances the meaning of our lives, and creates a climate for many kinds of believers to thrive together side by side. But mostly, we do it because it lasts. The seeds of charity are tenacious and cannot help but grow, no matter what poor soil they land in. We are—in our paltry and defective ways—trying to spread the light of Christ. He is the Light of the World. We share the Light of the World when we love. The world needs light and love. It's that simple.

CHAPTER 8

It's Meant to Be Fun

8

Despite the complexity and hard work of improving the world, there can be a deep sense of fulfillment and enjoyment. Food, sports, music, and serving together are all elements that enhance the fun and bonding we feel with each other. These activities connect us because they require cooperation, and humans have been cooperating for millennia in these ways because it's fun.

It's All About the Food

It was my first day on the job, and I was sitting through a dry HR orientation when the door swung open and in walked Gustavo Estrada. He took one look around and started cracking jokes. He sat next to me, and we realized we would be working in the same department. He declared we would be twins—born into our jobs on the same day. This made me smile because he and I were contrasting opposites in many ways. Soon the presenter was laughing, and all of us were suddenly having a good time.

Gustavo was from Gilroy, California—the garlic capital of the world (he never failed to mention that). Before Gilroy, Chicago. Before that, Guatemala City. He was dazzling at weaving humor, languages, food, culture, and exuberant friendliness into figurative snug coats and soft blankets that warmed people up.

He reveled in his Guatemalan culture. He sponsored salsa contests in our offices—which he usually won, but he shared his recipes with everyone. He brought Guatemalan hot chocolate to boring meetings. Every Thanksgiving, he would suggest a new appetizer recipe for me to try, guaranteed to impress my notoriously sniffy family. He made hundreds of tamales before Christmas and brought some for the office lunch on the first day of the new year. He cooked Guatemalan specialties of chile verde pork and then sold the dinners to raise money for his neighborhood robotics club.

He and I taught employment workshops together, for which he invented a fictional snow-cone shop facetiously called *Sno Way, Jose* so the class could practice making Jose's balance sheet add up. He would end the class by bringing a snow cone machine and serving up treats for the class.

When Gustavo heard that a relative of mine had adopted twin boys from Guatemala, he followed the twins' growing up with great interest. When they were twelve years old, he invited Max and Joe over to cook in his kitchen, inducting them into his special kitchen techniques. He called the twins his "cousins" and presented them with his secret recipe book. In addition to the *pepián* they dined on, the boys were being nourished about their country of origin in a way that fed a hunger they didn't know they had.

When I visited Gustavo the week he died, I wasn't surprised to see a Dead End street sign his son had gifted him propped up near his recliner. Gustavo thought it was hilarious. He could no longer eat, and that was the only thing that wasn't funny. Gustavo knew a secret about human beings—it's always about the food. He used food as currency to make every person feel warm, rich, and wanted.

Like Gustavo, Antoinette Kazan garnishes her volunteerism with food and has for thirty-five years. Antoinette was a young social worker in 1983. Into her neighborhood in Beirut, Lebanon, trickled men and women who had fled the civil war raging in the mountains. The people were hungry and exhausted. Antoinette asked her father if she could invite them into his house and feed them lunch. He agreed. Soon they were feeding twenty and then fifty people every day.

Her father bought the property next door and built a large kitchen and dining room. They named it Restaurant du Coeur—restaurant of the heart. Their idea was that anyone was welcome to a hot meal, whatever their circumstance or situation, and they would sit at tables and be served as guests. Antoinette knew it might be the one time during the day that her guests would feel dignified and cared for.

On the day I visited to help prepare the meal, I worked in the kitchen, shredding lettuce for salad. A middle-aged woman next to me was peeling potatoes. I asked her how she knew Antoinette.

"I'm her accountant," she said, laughing.

A man working at the sink piped up, "I'm her lawyer!"

I soon realized that Antoinette had engaged every person in her circle, and they had been preparing meals together for more than twenty years. Antoinette presided over the kitchen and dining room herself. She handed out steaming plates of food and baskets of bread. She smiled at people and greeted her regulars with friendly banter.

After the meal was served and cleaned up, we kitchen volunteers finally sat down to eat and visit.

Next to me at the table, Antoinette declared her philosophy that guided all she had done for more than thirty-five years. "The people who come have left their things, their houses, their jobs, and their lives. They have lost people very dear to them. But they do not have to lose their dignity." Antoinette spent her life and career connecting displaced people with new friends in the community, and she did it serving one noon meal at a time.[1]

There are certain activities we do as humans that work only if we can stay within agreed-upon boundaries. The rules are obviously voluntary, but we follow them because the activity works out when we do, and nobody can have any fun if we don't. Cooking is one of these activities. Recipes succeed or fail depending on following instructions and techniques and then modifying the rules with creativity. How did human beings ever figure out that mixing sugar, milk, and powder from the cacao seed in just the right proportions would be so delectable? Eating well-executed recipes naturally fosters cooperation and strong relationships. Most of us have a Gustavo in our lives who brings the food and makes the party. It's fun. We enjoy it. We want to do it again . . . and again.

It's All About the Music

Music is another example of the ways human beings cooperate for enjoyment. It's critical for bands, musicians, and singers to listen carefully to one another to stay in tune, read the music in the same ways, follow the cues of the conductor, or understand the rhythm. When all those elements are cooperatively clicking, it produces tunes that get into our heads and won't let go. We wake up with music. We drive with music. We dance the night away or pay big money to enjoy ourselves with music. Music is so powerful that it has well-documented healing qualities.

The cooperative nature and strong relationships that develop through playing music, enjoying music, and singing together play significant roles in responding to crises.

I planned a trip to London to attend the Windsor Dialogue conference on refugee resilience and invited my sister to join me. At one of the formal dinners, she was seated next to Michael Bochmann, and she asked him what he did for a living. He didn't say he was a violin virtuoso who has recorded and played in the finest concert halls in the world or that he directs world-class orchestras and ensembles. Instead, he humbly told her he was a music teacher.

Michael is a top-tier musician with a passion for helping other people express themselves in music. Spend just a few minutes with him and he will describe his delight in working with inner-city London school choirs that perform for tourists queuing outside the Tower of London. Or he will tell you of his latest trip with the AMAR Foundation to Kurdish, Iraq, to play music with Yazidis.

The Yazidis have practiced their ancient faith for literally thousands of years, living on their ancestral lands around the Syrian, Iraqi, and Iranian borders. The minority religion has often been misunderstood by Christianity and Islam as well as various political rulers. When ISIS fighters swept south out of Syria into Iraq in 2014, they brutally targeted the Yazidi population. Thousands were killed, and thousands of others were taken into sexual trafficking. Even now, many women and girls remain in captivity, but some have escaped or been rescued.

Music is central to Yazidi religion and culture, but it has never been written down or recorded. Michael worked closely with the Yazidi spiritual council, Yazidi musicians, and the AMAR Foundation to record their ancient musical traditions and preserve the archive in Oxford University's Bodleian Library.

He also worked to make Yazidi traditional and religious music more available to the displaced population by donating instruments and teaching hundreds of young musicians to play them in the camps where they still lived.

Michael described the joy the students felt when their traditional instruments were brought into the camps for them to play. "It's extraordinary how they've grown in confidence. The great thing about music is that it makes you live in the here and now. More than any other art form, it can make you happy in the present moment."[2]

Recently, Michael helped arrange for a Yazidi choir of women who had formerly been enslaved by ISIS to perform their sacred music in Westminster Abbey. I carefully watched the women's faces in that setting and observed the tangible relief the music provided for them as they sang. The women described singing as a healing act, and I could see that it was true. Michael staked his substantial reputation on the premise that music must be performed not just by professional musicians in expensive concert halls but also by ordinary people in everyday settings as balm, enjoyment, consolation, worship, entertainment, a bridge, and an old friend.

Baroness Emma Nicholson is a British politician and a close friend of Michael Bochmann's. As a member of the House of Lords and the founder and chair of the AMAR Foundation, she has worked continually to offer mental healthcare combined with music to people experiencing conflict and war. Her work in Iraq and Romania over nearly four decades documents that healing from trauma can occur through social integration and the consolation and discipline of music. Her philosophy recognizes that healing almost always starts from within and that uncovering the confidence to heal is at the heart of recovery for those whose development has been derailed by violence and trauma.

> "Like many people, music is the heart of the lives of the Yezidis, and indeed it is also the way they have worshiped the Almighty. They are worshippers of God, just like the rest of us. And like many of us, they use music for much of their praying.[3]
>
> "Every cluster of humanity contains within it the seeds of its own growth. How to uncover the seeds? We look for skills and competencies; we look for devotion

and dedication; we look for compassion, unselfishness, and humility; and we try to find and develop those talents to prompt healing."[4]

It's All About the Games

I have observed many times the power of sports in unifying individuals from different backgrounds and opinions so that by working together, they can play a game they love. The game can be chess, boules, basketball, or soccer—it doesn't matter.

The Catholic bishop and the local branch of Caritas in Florence, Italy, sponsored a fútbol league for the many African migrants whose asylum cases were in limbo. They were not eligible to work until their status was resolved, and they were sometimes quarreling with each other in boredom and frustration. Teams were assigned mixing tribe and country affiliations. Uniforms were issued that had a surprising unifying effect on men from so many different nationalities.

Once they stepped foot on the field, a new respect began to form among the players as they noted each other's abilities and began trusting each other as teammates. They were introduced to the community in Florence, not as migrants but as teams in the local fútbol league, which proved to be very positive. The unity among the teammates grew faster than any lecture or training could produce. They were having fun with each other and with the community, and the by-product was reduced conflict and new respect.

One of my favorite stories about the unifying power of sports comes from President Nelson Mandela of South Africa.

Nelson Mandela was imprisoned for twenty-four years. He spent eighteen of those years in a tiny cell in the highest-security prison. He was permitted only one guest each year and allowed to write one letter every six months. After he'd been released and received political power, it would have been very tempting to give vent to bitterness and retaliation.

Rugby was always known as the white Afrikaners' sport, and in the days of political struggle, it became a symbol of the ruling apartheid. The Black population of South Africa favored fútbol, so they would cheer noisily against the Springbok national rugby team as part of their political protest.

For all these reasons, it couldn't have been more shocking when President Mandela, having been democrat-ically elected only the year before as the first Black South African to ascend to the presidency, donned a green-and-gold Springbok hat and jacket and walked onto the pitch at the 1995 World Cup final to wish the Springboks good luck. He didn't just cheer the team. He learned every player's name, playing position, and history. It wasn't simply a photo op; he made himself into a true fan of the favored sport of his oppressors.

Francois Pienaar was the captain of the Springbok team, which won the world championship in that tournament. He described his feelings about what President Mandela managed to do.

"[Mandela was] one of the greatest leaders ever. He understood the power of sport. And he was brave enough to embrace the power of sport . . . as a changer. . . . What [Mandela] did is he got the whole nation to start supporting the team, you know. . . . And we realized as the tournament progressed, it's much more than just the tournament. It became much more than just a game.[5]

"Sport is a release mechanism, it's something that made us really proud. And when he walked into the dressing room wearing a Springbok on his heart, it was just, wow. . . . I couldn't sing the anthem because I knew I would cry. I was just so proud to be a South African that day."[6]

President Mandela was savvy enough to wield sport as a national unifier, beginning his quest at a rugby tournament.

It's All About the Service

People often say that they serve to make a difference or to feel better about themselves. Sometimes they serve to support an organization or cause they feel strongly about, or they want to learn something new. Often, they are hoping to develop personally or professionally through their service, or they enjoy meeting other people. But no matter why we start serving, there comes a moment when voluntary service gets inside our hearts and begins to change us in profoundly positive ways. Service can be addicting, but unlike substance addictions that isolate and break apart mental health, service can create bonds of trust and connection with others, and instead of a fleeting euphoria, service inspires long-term esteem and confidence that bolsters mental health. Plus, it's just fun.

Meagan Bjorklund is from Nampa, Idaho. Suicide is a multigenerational heartbreak in her family, and by age twelve, she was already reacting to crippling anxiety. Among a variety of clinical methods her family pursued to address her mental health, Meg describes the impact regular volunteering had on her as she worked through those feelings.

> Anxiety was a huge factor for me, and it eventually rolled over into depression and isolation. I know it's normal to feel anxiety when moving schools, where everything is new, but it just got worse for me. It's disgusting, but in middle school, I used to lock myself in a bathroom stall just to eat my lunch.

I didn't want anyone to approach me. I didn't want to look friendly. I just wanted to be left alone. I wanted to be a little scary. I felt scary on the outside and on the inside, and my appearance showed that. I couldn't get out of my own thoughts.

Our family got involved in service as part of our weekly routine. The volunteering was a distraction from all that stuff going on with us.

I was always anxious before every service project—I didn't want to go. But my mom would encourage me to try with a positive attitude and give it a shot. I was always relieved by the end of it because it felt much more relaxed than how I thought it would go. It became easier and easier to talk to people in general. It really just took practice, honestly. What kept me going back was the way I felt afterward—almost like a "service high." It's a feeling I didn't have anywhere else. It wasn't the only thing I was doing to strengthen my mental health, but it really helped to heal what I was going through emotionally at the time.

One of my favorite places to volunteer was visiting an elderly care center. I felt I could relate to the struggles the residents had gone through as they told me their stories. Most of them were very lonely and needed someone to talk to. I always left feeling good. I knew the person I talked to felt loved and heard, and I had connected with them. If I could help others feel like they were worth something, then maybe I was worth something too.

My life did not feel peaceful, but when I was helping others feel a little bit of peace and safety and comfort in their lives, I started to feel that way as well. It rubbed off on me, I guess. When I started acting like Jesus, that's when I found Him.

It wasn't easy and it took time—years—for me to really feel my own worth and that I had a purpose. It was very difficult to push through, but I am so thankful I did. I wouldn't be here otherwise.[7]

Food, music, sports, and service are natural bridges that bond groups because they are, essentially, fun to do. These enjoyable activities don't function without a certain order and discipline, so they help us want to work together to take the necessary ordered steps. They produce connection, friendly competition, satisfaction, and new respect—and those are bridges we like to walk over.

Robert Putnam is an American academic who published a book in 2000 called *Bowling Alone*. It was a plea for Americans to revive the culture of joining clubs because of its strong correlation to creating trust and positive social capital. He writes about "social bonding" among people who share many common traits and "social bridging" practiced with people who have many differences. Of the two, social bridging is harder but more necessary. Sports and service clubs offer many opportunities for social bridging. His premise twenty-five years ago was that increased social capital would save American democracy, but he has a new caveat after the passage of years.

> It's got to be fun. I mean, building social capital is not like castor oil—"you've got to take it because it's good for you, even though it feels awful." It ought to be fun. I am famous as the advocate of bowling clubs, but you don't bowl so you can build a better community, you bowl because it's fun. And in the doing of the bowling, in a team, you're hanging out with folks and sometimes you're talking about the latest TV show, or occasionally you might talk about the garbage pickup in town. And that's democracy. . . . Don't think the way to save democracy is just to set out to save democracy.[8]

If you agree with Putnam that American culture is growing lonelier and you are interested in creating more connection in your own life, here are four experiments to try.

FOOD	SPORTS
Host your nearest neighbors for a potluck, and ask each to describe why they chose the dish they brought.	Sign up for a sport you do not play well and simply enjoy learning the skills the way you did as a child.
MUSIC	**SERVICE**
Ask someone fifteen years younger than you to curate a playlist of six of their favorite songs and then listen to and talk about them together.	Meet with your local school principal about their priorities. Organize a neighborhood service project to help.

Gustavo's Hilachas

(slow-cooked beef stew)

> 1 lb flank steak
>
> salt
>
> pepper
>
> 1 Tbsp olive oil

SAUCE

> 1 medium onion, diced
>
> 3 bay leaves
>
> 2 large Roma tomatoes, diced
>
> 4 large husked tomatillos, diced

1 cup red bell pepper, diced

1 yellow onion, sliced

2 cloves of garlic, minced

1 Guajillo chile, remove the seeds

1 Ancho chile, remove the seeds

4 cups beef stock

Salt and pepper flank steak, and brown on all sides using a bit of olive oil in a preheated saucepan. After the meat is browned, place it in a slow cooker with the sauce ingredients. Slow cook on low for 7 hours. Remove the meat, and discard the bay leaves. Let the meat cool briefly, and then shred by cutting against the grain, and set aside. Reserve the liquid and puree it.

ADD

3 corn tortillas—toasted and then crumbled into the sauce.

Break off ¼ block of achiote paste

1 Goya Sazón seasoning packet

4 medium potatoes, diced

In a saucepan over medium heat, simmer the sauce until it is a nice, thick consistency. Add the tortillas, achiote paste, and Goya Sazón seasoning. Blend again using an immersion blender. Add the potatoes. Let the flavors blend. The sauce should be like a thick meat stew.

If it is too thin, cook it down longer. If it is too thick, add some beef stock or water.

Add the shredded meat to create the finished stew. This serves beautifully with slightly cooked snipped green beans.

Listen to Michael Bochmann perform Ralph Vaughan Williams's "The Lark Ascending" with the English Symphony Orchestra at Gloucester Cathedral, with young musicians from around Gloucestershire here:

https://shdwmtn.com/vaughan

Listen to the Yazidi Ashty Women's
Peace Choir perform here:

https://shdwmtn.com/Amar

https://shdwmtn.com/yazidi

Some Final Lessons on What Can and Cannot Be Done

9

The Common Good Is
Our Common Interest

Late in President Jimmy Carter's presidency, high energy costs, runaway inflation, and his inability to resolve the Iranian hostage crisis made it clear that he would not be elected to a second term. He was supposed to give a national speech about developing alternative energy sources, but he sensed it would just cycle through the news, the same old thing. Instead, he canceled the speech and, after a few days, decided to address the nation on a completely different subject. He went out on a limb, unvarnished and frank, to talk about what happens to a nation when it becomes every man or woman for themselves. He felt this was at the root of our national problems and wanted to bring it before the country whether his political advisers thought it was smart to do or not.

Carter felt deeply troubled about the circumstances in the nation. Democratic society cannot function for long if only a small percentage of people are succeeding and prospering. When individuals and institutions begin grabbing for their own advantage at the expense of others, it poisons the idea of the common good. It leads to fragmentation and self-interest. The fact that this speech was given in 1979 makes Carter seem as if he were reading the twenty-first century writ large.

PRESIDENT JIMMY CARTER

"I want to talk to you right now about a fundamental threat to American democracy. . . . It is a crisis of confidence. It is a crisis that strikes at the very heart and soul and spirit of our national will. We can see this crisis in the growing doubt about the meaning of our own lives and in the loss of our unity of purpose for our nation. . . .

"We've always had a faith that the days of our children would be better than our own. Our people are losing that faith, not only in government itself but in the ability as citizens to serve as the ultimate rulers and shapers of our democracy. . . .

"These changes did not happen overnight. They've come upon us gradually over the last generation, years that were filled with shocks and tragedy. We were sure that ours was a nation of the ballot, not the bullet, until the murders of John [F.] Kennedy, Robert [F.] Kennedy, and Martin Luther King Jr. We were taught that our armies were always invincible and our causes were always just, only to suffer the agony of Vietnam. We respected the presidency as a place of honor until the shock of Watergate. . . . These wounds are still very deep. They have never been healed. . . .

"We know the strength of America. We are strong. We can regain our unity. We can regain our confidence. We are the heirs of generations who survived threats much more powerful and awesome than those that challenge us now. . . . We are at a turning point in our history. There are two paths to choose. One is a path I've warned about tonight, the path that leads to fragmentation and self-interest. Down that road lies a mistaken idea of freedom, the right to grasp for ourselves some advantage over others.

"All the traditions of our past, all the lessons of our heritage, all the promises of our future point to another path—the path of common purpose and the restoration of American values. . . .

"In closing, let me say this: I will do my best, but I will not do it alone. Let your voice be heard. Whenever you have a chance, say something good about our country. With God's help, and for the sake of our nation, it is time for us to join hands in America.[1]

"We are all Americans together, and we must not forget that the common good is our common interest and our individual responsibility."[2]

I let that last phrase ring in my head. The common good is our common interest and our individual responsibility. I can live up to my individual responsibility and build on my personal privilege to find common ground with others. I can work shoulder to shoulder with them to restore faith, heal wounds, and build bridges. These are things I can do.

I can get involved in local issues. I can donate money where I have confidence that it will advance the work of trusted networks. I can advocate with my local and national government and raise my voice on behalf of those who cannot raise their voices. I can live my life with a gracious respect for others who are different from me. I can learn about current events and gather others to work on productive solutions. I can take the next generation with me as we learn together.

We can't let self-interest or inertia stop us from working for the common good as we see it. The difficulties are real, but we have done much and can do much more to improve society and make it safer, healthier, more equitable, and more enjoyable. The power is in us.

There Is Suffering We Can Soften

Being active in our communities will soon reveal that there are situations we cannot immediately resolve, but we can soften the negative effects.

I first met Yotam Polizer during the Japan earthquake, tsunami, and nuclear disaster in 2011. Yotam is a man of great empathy and energy. So many people in that disaster lost their lives, homes, and livelihoods. Besides the tremendous damage from the 9.1 earthquake and the tsunami that followed, there was great anxiety and concern about the nuclear plant and the possible radiation people might be exposed to.[3] Yotam is the CEO for IsraAid, and their specialty was to train counselors who could help individuals process post-traumatic stress from a disaster.

Post-traumatic stress is a condition that results in a series of emotional and physical reactions in individuals who have either witnessed or experienced a traumatic event, such as a disaster, a conflict, or violent experiences.[4] When the emotion and recall of a very big experience are bottled up inside a person, they are flooded with adrenaline at random times and can't sleep or wake up with memories and flashbacks that feel as if they are reliving the event. However, there are ways to guide traumatic experiences and open the door to emotional growth if the experience is processed in healthy ways.

Looking back on the Japanese disaster, Yotam reflected:

> "From Fukushima to Afghanistan, from the Ebola outbreak in Sierra Leone to the Syrian refugee crisis—and very strongly after the trauma of October 7 in both Israel and Gaza—I've seen . . . the ability of communities and individuals to reach post-traumatic growth. I truly believe that our role as helpers is to help the most vulnerable communities work together toward post-traumatic growth. There is always an opportunity for it, especially in the worst crises."[5]

To help process post-traumatic stress, IsraAid leads three practices that have proved effective in helping people heal. If the three practices are done correctly, post-traumatic stress can slowly subside, and post-traumatic growth can take its place. The basic elements for growth are these:

1. **Talk to a trained person** who has the skills to help you process what happened to you. Very often, the experience is too big for words, and so counselors use art, music, nature, or massage to identify the triggers and talk through the emotions and experiences in a safe way.

2. **Take control.** Decide ahead of time something you will do that takes away the power and stress when the dreams come or the adrenaline surges. It could be something like taking a walk outdoors, counting your breaths, or finding a friend.

3. **Help others.** When a person has successfully processed their own stress, they often make the most empathetic and credible counselors to help others. After the earthquake and tsunami in Japan, IsraAid and other organizations gave professional training to Japanese community members so they could seek out others who were still suffering from post-traumatic stress and help them as well. The cycle of help grew bigger and bigger as more and more people processed their trauma and reached out to others. There are always situations we cannot change. We all experience a measure of traumatic stress from the events in our lives. But if we can process tragedies into empathy and take control of our responses, we put ourselves in a position to help other people. When we follow through from our own experiences and help others—even as we are healing ourselves—growth occurs. We become more sensitive to

suffering, more resilient to stress, more empathetic toward others, more able to bring about change.

Our personal efforts can soften the suffering of others and create growth for them and us. But at other times, we need to make sure we are doing okay ourselves. The work of helping others through emotional crises creates baggage that we tend to carry with us.

Along with Multiplying, We Need to Replenish

Lloyd was my boss. In 1999, I was a new humanitarian analyst assigned to work with him. Our geographic area covered Europe and the Middle East, and we were severely understaffed. He met with me every morning for twenty minutes. Those twenty minutes were a whirlwind of activity as he gave me a list of tasks I would report back on the next day.

He edited the projects I wrote, cutting out the extra words. He rattled off a list of books and articles I should read. But most of all, he took an interest in me and my professional development. I was overworked and had stacks of projects on my desk that needed completing or filing. But Lloyd knew something I didn't know at the time: Humanitarian projects aren't the real work. Building people is the real work—and he was building me.

He would often have me come in and listen to him converse on the phone. At first, I was exasperated. I thought it was a waste of time for me to sit there and listen to the conversation that was about his work and not mine. After he would hang up, he would debrief with me. What had I heard? What concern was unexpressed? What did I think should happen next? It didn't take me long to learn this was valuable.

Lloyd often started our morning off with a question such as, What do you know about Palestinian influence in Jordanian politics? So I wasn't very surprised when I went to visit him at his home and he greeted me with, "What's your understanding of the biblical injunction to multiply and replenish the earth?" It was a funny question to ask a single woman in her fifties. I didn't know where he was going with this question. But it turned out Lloyd was about to give me one of the most helpful lessons of my professional career.

Lloyd had pancreatic cancer by then and didn't have long to live. He had been thoughtful about my visit and had some comments written on a legal pad. We both knew this was probably the last time we would see each other. And he wanted to talk about multiplying and replenishing.

"It's not just about having children," he told me.

These are the notes I made in Lloyd's own words:

Multiplying—*is taking all of our talents and using them to bless other people's lives.*

Replenishing—*is finishing something and then stepping back to rest and celebrate what was accomplished.*

He confessed to me his reaction when I took a sabbatical from work and lived in France for a year. *"I thought privately, 'Well, that's a stupid idea.' You stepped away for a year from your career and everything else. I thought, 'Okay, that sounds great, but I could never do that.' In hindsight now, I think it was a wonderful thing you did. I see now it was absolutely critical. You multiplied, and then you replenished. I should have done more of that in my life."*

You can see from just the bit I've shared that Lloyd was a magnifier of the highest order. He multiplied his talents and used them to bless other people until the day he died. Lloyd was also a replenisher, though not as much as he wished.

He couldn't sit still—lying on a beach was torture for him—but he loved being out in nature. He went for a run every morning in the predawn light of his neighborhood streets. He would often pray for people as he ran by their house. He grew up on a cattle ranch and, even after I knew him, looked forward to rounding up and sorting cattle every fall. He liked camping out on the trail and hiking;

that was a sacred time for him. He loved philosophical and religious discussions with friends. He was deeply devoted to his family. It gave him great energy to learn new things and teach others what he had learned.

In the spirit of Lloyd as a teacher, as a builder, as a man with spiritual questions, let me share the last advice he gave me written on a legal pad for me to take home.

> Now that I'm dying, this is the advice I would pass on to everyone. Take a look at this balance between giving and receiving, this balance between multiplying and replenishing, this balance of taking care of others and taking care of yourself. Let's work hard but then let's celebrate what we've done. Let's replenish, re-think, re-engage with the Lord and ask Him: "What project would you like me to work on next?" We have to take care of ourselves. Multiplying and replenishing is all connected—a whole piece. The equal exchange of our energy.
>
> Genesis 2:1-3 says "and the heaven and the earth were finished, all the host of them, And on the seventh day God ended his work . . . and . . . rested . . . from all his work which he had made. And God blessed the seventh day, and sanctified it."[6]

It isn't indulgent or luxurious to replenish ourselves. It is a divine commandment.

There Are Places We Cannot Reach and Situations We Cannot Control

In my experience, learning to care for people progresses along a spectrum. You start off in the early stages with a bleeding heart, saying, "I'm going to give them stuff. I'm going to get involved because I have a thing that they don't, and I will give it to them." It's born partly from guilt and largely from a sincere desire to help. But as you move along the spectrum by experience, you begin to realize, "I have something to offer people, and the people have something to offer me. This is really an exchange where we both benefit." People I consider poor may not have physical goods, but they have characteristics I don't have that benefit me. At that point, it becomes less about the physical things and more about an exchange.

Much good can be done along the spectrum, but it's important to recognize, through a great many experiences, that at the end of the spectrum, there are always issues, mostly the biggest issues, that you cannot do anything about. They are entrenched in politics and geographic distance. They happen because of the fury of nature or the fury of men. I do not have the power to change them, no matter how much I want to. I feel sickened to see destruction and death—dreams going up in smoke from smart bombs, futures defaulting for generations because of prejudice and firepower. I despair to see the needless suffering, grief, and cruelty that we cause for each other.

When I am overwhelmed like this, two things help me: Number one, I go small. I cannot stop the war in Sudan, but I can befriend a Sudanese person. I cannot restore all that is lost in Gaza or Israel, but I can share the promise of peace at Yom Kippur, Ramadan, or Easter. I try to find a small thing that I can do with power.

Number two, I pray. I'm a woman who believes in prayer. There is a New Testament verse in the Book of James that reads: *"Confess your faults one to another, and pray one for another, that ye may be healed. The effectual fervent prayer of a righteous [person] availeth much"* (James 5:16). I can pray for the people I will never be able to reach. I can pour out my heart and ask the God of heaven to bless them and open doors to them. I hope to God that prayer avails much. It is too often the only recourse left.

Shortly before the latest conflict in Israel and Gaza started, I crossed over from Jerusalem into Bethlehem to visit a place called the Milk Grotto. Nearby, I entered a sanctuary and saw a nun dressed in a white robe with a black veil kneeling at an altar in an empty room. I learned that a Catholic organization had built sanctuaries in twelve locations of conflict around the world. In this one, like the others, a rotation of nuns took turns kneeling and praying for peace around the clock. That kind of dedication and trust in the power of prayer touched me. It is an acknowledgment that after we cheerfully do all that lies within our power, we can then stand still with the utmost assurance that God will answer prayers and move on behalf of the poor.

I am not a nun, but I join those sisters in praying for peace and reconciliation. I believe God weeps over what we have allowed to happen on this beautiful earth He gave us. Most often, His intervention does not come immediately. He gives us a chance to correct for ourselves what we have done, but we know He has undertaken to make all things right—in this world and in the next. That is the

promise of faith, the evidence of things we cannot see (see Hebrews 11:1). We rail against waiting; we want to change the world so that it will not be like this anymore. I hope we can. I hope we do. But the acceptance of what cannot be done lies at the other end of the spectrum: an acknowledgment of our limitations and a trust in God. He is not indifferent to us and our misery. He has already given His Son, who paid for our horrors with His own blood. I trust in the day when Jesus will give all who suffered so endlessly beauty for their ashes.

In summary:

- We can act. Our efforts and gifts make a concrete difference. There are people we can know and actions we can take that will translate into greater relief, more unity, and more justice.
- There is suffering we cannot remove, but we can soften it and help it transform from pain into growth.
- There are opportunities for multiplying our efforts, and there are times to replenish, celebrate, and care for ourselves.
- And there are things we can do nothing about except pray, the highest form of help we can offer another.

The Work Is Now Yours

10

Lao Tzu, the Chinese philosopher and founder of Taoism, has a famous quote:

> "As for the best leaders, people do not notice their existence.
>
> The next best, the people honor and praise.
>
> The next, the people fear; And the next, the people hate.
>
> . . . But when the best leaders' work is done, the people say, 'We did it ourselves.'"[1]

This book was my attempt to demonstrate the principles of action that, in the end, allow communities and families to say, "We did it ourselves." I hope you are encouraged to take part in more informed action. The stories I've told and the people in them aren't perfect, but they are individuals acting for themselves and not simply being acted upon by outside forces. The individuals I wrote about weren't afraid to try something and then improve it. That's how everything meaningful starts.

I said in the introduction that answering the question "How can I help?" was the point of the book. I've tried to shed light on core principles so you can ask yourself more nuanced questions instead:

- How can I help people in the ways they want to be helped?
- How does my help allow others to eventually do for themselves?
- What help can I offer that confronts root causes?
- What about when I cannot help?

I hope you no longer believe you are too isolated or your efforts are too small to make a difference in a life, with a child, in a hurting community, in a skeptical world.

For reference, here are the twelve principles I used in the chapters:

1. You are most powerful where you live
2. Find local solutions for local problems
3. Trusted networks determine the success of the money
4. The right questions reveal the real answers
5. Everyone is rich and has something to offer
6. Protect dignity, protect choice
7. My solution to your problem will always be wrong

8. Real help is always an exchange
9. Spend energy attacking root causes
10. Sustainability—what happens when the problem comes up next time?
11. Volunteerism weaves social fabric and can be a tool for peace
12. It's meant to be fun

If you're looking for a place to start, here are fifty ideas that can spark you into action right away. Once again, Mother Teresa is unerringly right: "We must know that we have been created for greater things, not just to be a number in the world, not just to go for diplomas and degrees, this work and that work. We have been created in order to love and to be loved." Start anywhere you feel the zing.

50 Prompts to Get Started

1. Cultivate a sincere friendship with someone older or younger than you.
2. Talk to your mayor or city council about their priorities and how you might help.
3. Try participating in another faith's holiday or practice.
4. Learn a new skill from someone else.
5. Introduce yourself to a neighbor you don't know.
6. Debate the other side of one of your favorite political issues.

7. Who are the newest people in your community? Where did they come from? What do they like? What can they teach you? What are their pressing issues?

8. Teach a new skill to someone who wants to learn.

9. Never let a problem to be solved be more important than a person to be loved.

10. Resolve a conflict in your life.

11. Pray for the people you see on the news.

12. Invite someone from another faith or viewpoint to do something with you.

13. Smile in your liver—that general, benign attitude you emanate that you can be trusted.

14. Volunteer for a project on JustServe. Take a friend.

15. What is making your community inaccessible? What needs changing?

16. Learn about what is served in your school for lunch and the decisions behind it.

17. What is your community's emergency plan? How will people know what to do?

18. Talk to medical providers at your local low-income clinic. What are their urgent needs?

19. Post a project on JustServe.

20. Respond to rudeness with kindness.

21. Put your phone away and interact with people by looking in their eyes.

22. Read a book aloud with someone.

23. Give books as gifts, and share why you chose that particular book for the person.

24. Start a recipe-sharing group for new ways to prepare and love healthy foods or holiday foods or foods from another culture.

25. Identify an opportunity to focus on cooperation instead of competition.

26. Keep your promises; be a person of your word.

27. Research the specific reasons food insecurity might be on the rise in your community. What impacts does it have? How might it be changed?

28. Attend a town hall or city council meeting.

29. Volunteer to read to a school class or at the library.

30. Help a child with homework after school.

31. Find out what barriers in your community are restricting new mothers from accessing prenatal care. What can be done to improve access?

32. Cook with kids, and let them make decisions about how meals are prepared.

33. Plant a garden and share your produce.

34. Walk in a naturally beautiful place and feel the connection to the earth and sky. Invite someone to walk with you.

35. Ensure a private place and supportive environment at the office, workplace, campus, house of worship, and

other public venues for mothers who breastfeed or pump.

36. Read a book or article about an issue you don't support.

37. Support local lending libraries and other resources for good books.

38. Work with your local government to ensure your community's water and food sources are free from contaminants and impurities.

39. Grow something from a seed.

40. Read aloud, play music, or sing at a senior center.

41. Write or visit your congressional representative; tell them what is important to you.

42. What are the maternal and infant mortality rates at your local hospital? What actions could the community take to improve them?

43. Be a mentor to students at the local junior high or high school. What do they dream of doing? What options for their future can you discover together?

44. Volunteer at a community kitchen sometime other than the holidays.

45. Convene a neighborhood council; choose an issue to address together.

46. Role-play mock interviews with graduating seniors or job seekers.

47. Donate business clothing to the local YWCA or YMCA.
48. Build your local economy—hire local, shop local. Look to support new businesses.
49. Invite an international student for a meal or activity with your family.
50. Find one new person to interact with. Every day.

I end the book with a plea. Share what you are doing. Contribute your own unique, quirky brand of goodness to the collective whole. Include others in your passion projects. Discover the aspirations tucked inside people you respect or those you want to get to know better. Meet with government and other leaders, and let them know what is important to you and what you are willing to do. Flood social media with the stories of people who are changing their own interiors and then overhauling their exterior environments. If you want to join other readers of this book and see what they are doing, you can use the hashtag #SmallThingsGreatLove or #SmallActsBigImpact.

The rest of the work is yours.

Sharon Eubank

The Trusted Networks
Where You Have Influence

One day, I took the ferry to Catalina Island, off the coast of Southern California. It was winter, and the town was quiet in the off-season without many tourists, but I noticed this sign in the main square of Avalon, the largest town. With approximately 4,200 citizens, the island has a rich tradition of trusted networks.

You may not initially think that you belong to many trusted networks, but your interests, your relations, your school affiliations, and your geography all create overlapping circles of influence that are the bread and butter of how you engage at the local level.

Which of your networks have the greatest ability to influence the community? What might you do to increase trust among the members of your networks?

Your Personal Foundational Support Beams

In Chapter 1, I described the five steel beams that give weight to my personal approach to service:

- Universal human rights
- The fundamentals of humanitarian action
- True service is motivated purely by love
- Service opportunities build stronger character in givers and receivers
- We are all brothers and sisters, children of a loving God

What are the deeply held values that make up your own foundational support beams? How do you articulate them in a way that builds common ground with others? You can write them in the graphic or describe them in the space below.

_____

_____

_____

_____

_____

Building a Service Resume

https://www.justserve.org/
smallthingsgreatlove

JustServe not only connects people to local volunteer opportunities, but over time they can also use it to generate a service résumé that will record the scope of your volunteer experiences.

Perhaps you want to include your service résumé on a school application or professional bio. Maybe you simply want to feel the accomplishment of doing good work. Whatever the motivation, registering on JustServe allows you to create a profile of personal interests, receive suggestions for relevant projects, and celebrate your volunteer milestones over time.

Use the QR code above to connect to the digital resource, or jot your first experiences here to begin a résumé and just serve!

Date	Organization	Activity	Hours Spent

Finding a New Perspective

This famous photo called *Earthrise* was taken by Apollo 8 astronaut Bill Anders in 1968. He had been photographing lunar craters when he saw the Earth rise from the horizon of the moon. He turned and quickly snapped the iconic photo.

Earthrise was the first time human beings could view our home from a different perspective. Petty clashes and disputed borders fell away. The Earth appeared as a singular blue jewel set in a sparkling cosmic necklace. The majesty of Earth as a creation captivated the imagination of billions of people on that Christmas Eve in 1968 and feels even more powerful today.

There may not be a photo of the event, but you have also witnessed great shifts in perspective. What life events have drastically altered your views? What perspective shift would you grant to others if you could? Who is the person you know best who rises above petty differences and finds unifying themes in their work or life? What image would you capture to signify the place most dear or special to you?

_____

_____

_____

Notes

Introduction

1. "Golden Rule," Living Peace International, accessed February 4, 2025, http://livingpeaceinternational.org/en/the-project/330-regola-d-oro-2 .html.

Chapter 1: The Basics

1. Ernesto Sirolli, "Want to help someone? Shut up and listen!" TED Talk, Christchurch, Canterbury, NZ, September 2012, https://www .ted.com/talks/ernesto_sirolli_want_to_help_someone_shut_up_and _listen.
2. Allida Black, "Compelled to Act: Eleanor Roosevelt, A Fearful World and an International Vision of Human Rights," *UN Chronicle*, December 8, 2023, https://www.un.org/en/un-chronicle/compelled-act-eleanor -roosevelt-fearful-world-and-international-vision-human-rights.
3. Blanche Wiesen Cook, "Beacon of Hope – Eleanor Roosevelt and the Universal Declaration of Human Rights," anniversary film, December 8, 2018, by United Nations, YouTube, https://www.youtube.com /watch?v=Lp-3CQ6ZD4k&t=1s.
4. Eleanor Roosevelt, "Transcript of Speech on Human Rights" (1951), Franklin D. Roosevelt Presidential Library, https://www.fdrlibrary .org/documents/356632/390886/Eleanor+Roosevelt+Transcript+of +Speech+on+Human+Rights+1951.pdf.
5. "The Fundamental Principles of the International Red Cross and the Red Crescent Movement," ICRC, August 2015, https://www.icrc.org/sites /default/files/topic/file_plus_list/4046-the_fundamental_principles _of_the_international_red_cross_and_red_crescent_movement.pdf.

6. "Code of Conduct for the Movement and NGOs in Disaster Relief," IFRC, accessed February 4, 2025, https://www.ifrc.org/our-promise /do-good/code-conduct-movement-ngos.

7. History.com Editors, "Mother Teresa," History, February 26, 2024, https://www.history.com/topics/religion/mother-theresa.

8. Leah Hall, "54 Mother Teresa Quotes That Inspire Love, Faith, and Hope," *Country Living*, March 31, 2022, https://www.countryliving .com/life/a39155616/mother-teresa-quotes/,

9. See Wayne K. Hinton and Leonard J. Arrington, "Origin of the Welfare Plan of The Church of Jesus Christ of Latter-day Saints," *BYU Studies*, vol. 5 no. 2 (1964), 67–85, https://byustudies.byu.edu/article /origin-of-the-welfare-plan-of-the-church-of-jesus-christ-of-latter-day -saints/#note-233.

10. Special Meeting of Stake Presidencies, October 2, 1936, as quoted by Marion G. Romney, "Living Welfare Principles," *Ensign*, November 1981, 92.

11. "Our primary purpose was to set up, in so far as it might be possible, a system under which the curse of idleness would be done away with, the evils of a dole abolished, and independence, industry, thrift and self-respect be once more established amongst our people. The aim of the Church is to help the people to help themselves. Work is to be re-enthroned as the ruling principle of the lives of our Church member- ship" (Heber J. Grant, in *Conference Report*, Oct. 1936, 3).

12. Hinton and Arrington, "Origin of the Welfare Plan," https://byustudies .byu.edu/article/origin-of-the-welfare-plan-of-the-church-of-jesus-christ -of-latter-day-saints/#note-233.

Chapter 2: You Are Most Powerful Where You Live

1. "Best intentions: When disaster relief brings anything but relief," *Sun- day Morning*, CBS News, September 3, 2017, https://www.cbsnews .com/news/best-intentions-when-disaster-relief-brings-anything-but -relief.

2. "Best intentions," *Sunday Morning*, https://www.cbsnews.com/news /best-intentions-when-disaster-relief-brings-anything-but-relief/.

3. Dale Herzog, "Ever sent clothes, supplies or toys in response to a disas- ter? Here's what probably happened to it," We Humans, *Ideas*, TED. com, September 25, 2018, https://ideas.ted.com/after-a-disaster-dont -send-toys-or-clothing-send-money-heres-why/.

4. Herzog, "Ever sent clothes . . .," https://ideas.ted.com/after-a-disaster -dont-send-toys-or-clothing-send-money-heres-why/.

5. Herzog, "Ever sent clothes . . .," https://ideas.ted.com/after-a-disaster -dont-send-toys-or-clothing-send-money-heres-why/.

6. Emma Steven, "Meet the determined woman who invented duct tape," Johnson & Johnson, February 8, 2018, https://www.jnj.com/our-heritage /vesta-stoudt-the-woman-who-invented-duct-tape.

7. Allison Pond, "Special report: How Utah became one refugee family's final chance at survival," *Deseret News*, December 18, 2017, https://www .deseret.com/2017/12/19/20637543/special-report-how-utah-became -one-refugee-family-s-final-chance-at-survival.

8. "The Top 5 Things Your Child's Principal Wants You to Know," Studio 5 with Brooke Walker, September 9, 2022, https://studio5.ksl.com /5-things-your-childs-principal-wants-you-to-know/.

Chapter 3: Trusted Networks

1. See "Humanitarianism in Africa," Wikipedia, last modified August 29, 2024, https://en.wikipedia.org/wiki/Humanitarianism_in_Africa.

   "Since 1960, rich countries have sent over USD $2.6 trillion in aid to Africa. In the period between 1970 and 1998, when aid to Africa peaked, poverty rose from 11% to 66%. A significant cause of this rise in poverty has been the vast sums of foreign-based aid" ("Humanitarianism in Africa"). It inadvertently increased inequality, corruption, and conflict.

   Although emergency aid has helped prevent short-term suffering in Africa, systematic aid has harmed Africans by increasing corruption and poverty. Unconditional aid to Africa has been largely proliferated by corrupt officials who engage in private consumption instead of public investment. Aid-motivated corruption reduces investment, which, in the long-term, has suppressed many countries' economic growth. This lower growth has led to increased poverty in Africa, which causes donors to send more aid, creating a vicious cycle of aid and poverty.

2. See *Dambisa Moyo, Dead Aid: Why Aid Is Not Working and How There is a Better Way for Africa* (New York: Farrar, Straus and Giroux, 2009), 48–51.

3. Elizabeth Pierce, personal interview with author, August 8, 2024.

4. Pamela Atkinson, "A life of small miracles," interview by Lois M. Collins, *Deseret News*, April 19, 2021, https://www.deseret.com /indepth/2021/4/19/22392287/a-life-of-small-miracles-pamela -atkinson-utah-homelessness-crisis-religion-faith-service.

5. Raad Kelani, personal interview with author, November 2015.

6. Robert Hokanson, personal interview with author, April 29, 2019.

7. Stefano Battain, "Why is cash assistance a critical form of humanitarian aid?" International Rescue Committee, last updated August 15, 2023, https://www.rescue.org/article/why-cash-assistance-critical-form -humanitarian-aid.

8. Iffat Idris, "Conflict-sensitive cash transfers: unintended negative consequences," K4D, August 30, 2017, https://assets.publishing.service .gov.uk/media/59df6771e5274a11ac1c4964/200-Conflict-Sensitive -Cash-Transfers-Unintended-Negative-Consequences.pdf.
9. "Toa," The Bionicle Wiki, accessed February 4, 2025, https://bionicle .fandom.com/wiki/Toa_(2001).

Chapter 4· Asking the Right Questions

1. Thomas L. Friedman, "The Value of Listening," Opinion, *New York Times*, February 7, 2024, https://www.nytimes.com/live/2024/02/06/opinion /thepoint?smid=tw-nytopinion&smtyp=cur#friedman-blog-post.
2. Michael Nyenhuis, personal interview with author, April 5, 2024.
3. Nyenhuis, April 5, 2024.
4. "James P. Comer," Wikipedia, last updated October 21, 2024, https:// en.wikipedia.org/wiki/James_P._Comer.
5. "James P. Comer," *Great Pedagogical Thinkers*, Pedagogy For Change, https://www.pedagogy4change.org/james-p-comer-significant-learning.
6. Carlton Ashby, "The Power Is In *You*: Three Keys to Success – Relationships, Relationships, Relationships," Education World, 2008, https:// www.educationworld.com/a_admin/columnists/ashby/ashby001.shtml.
7. Alene Tchekmedyian, "Boy speaks out after sewer pipe rescue: 'I was just praying to God to help me and to not die,'" *Los Angeles Times*, April 2, 2018, https://www.latimes.com/local/lanow/la-me-ln-sewer -pipe-rescue-20180402-story.html.
8. Miguel Almaguer, "Boy who fell into LA sewer found alive," Nightly News, NBC, April 2, 2018, "https://www.nbcnews.com/nightly-news /video/boy-who-fell-into-la-sewer-found-alive-1200746051577.
9. "Boy, 13, rescued 12 hours after being swept into Los Angeles sewer system," *The Guardian*, April 2, 2018, https://www.theguardian.com /us-news/2018/apr/02/los-angeles-sewer-rescue-boy-sewage.
10. Nyenhuis, April 5, 2024.
11. Eran Hayet, personal interview with author, July 2023.
12. "Philippines Typhoon Facts and Figures," Disasters Emergency Committee, 2013, https://www.dec.org.uk/article/philippines-typhoon-facts -and-figures.
13. Danny Petilla, "Tzu Chi Foundation: Let's hear it for amazing Buddhist responders," Inquirer.net, November 9, 2014, https://globalnation.inquirer .net/114046/tzu-chi-foundation-lets-hear-it-for-amazing-buddhist -responders.
14. Ezra Taft Benson, "Born of God," *Ensign*, Nov. 1985, 6.

Chapter 5: Protecting Dignity

1. Brett MacDonald, personal interview with author, October 3, 2024.

2. Denis Estimon, "At one high school, no one eats lunch alone," *On the Road with Steve Hartman*, by CBS Evening News, YouTube, March 10, 2017, https://www.youtube.com/watch?v=QdDa2outstI.

3. Twila Bird, ed., *Let Me Tell You My Story: Refugee Stories of Hope, Courage, and Humanity* (Sanger, Calif.: Familius, 2018), 114.

4. Julie Rose, host, *Top of Mind with Julie Rose*, podcast, season 1, episode 545, "Refugees: Their Story Is Our Story," BYUradio, May 3, 2017, https://www.byuradio.org/ff414e7f-6c75-4c8d-ba4e-d6b6653add0d/top-of-mind-with-julie-rose-refugees-their-story-is-our-story.

5. Trisha Leimer, personal interview with author, September 9, 2024.

6. "Global Dignity Day Toolkit," Global Dignity, 2018, https://globaldignity.org/wp-content/uploads/2018/02/Global-Dignity-Day_Basic-Tool-Kit-2018.pdf.

7. Dion, "The Bakery That Gave an Ex-Inmate a Second Chance!" July 21, 2015, by Upworthy, YouTube, https://www.youtube.com/watch?v=pyI7pwbtNBo.

8. Brett G. Scharffs, Ján Figel, and Jane H. Wise, *Points of Light* (Provo, UT: The International Center for Law and Religious Studies, 2021), 31, https://www.dignityforeveryone.org/app/uploads/2023/04/20-396-Points-of-Light-Book-Jan2022.pdf.

9. "Speech delivered by Mr N R Mandela for the 'Make Poverty History' Campaign," Item 760, The Nelson Mandela Foundation Archive at the Centre of Memory, February 3, 2005, https://archive.nelsonmandela.org/index.php/za-com-mr-s-760.

10. Scharffs, Figel, and Wise, *Points of Light*, 89.

11. Eleanor Roosevelt, speech delivered at the presentation of "In Your Hands: A Guide for Community Action for the Tenth Anniversary of the Universal Declaration of Human Rights," March 27, 1958, United Nations, New York (cited in Scharffs, Figel, and Wise, *Points of Light*, 9). This statement by Eleanor Roosevelt is widely quoted without citation, both in UN materials and in other sources, and the UN Library and Archives have been asked about it many times over the years. We have not found the original source text of the speech. Part of the speech is quoted in a *New York Times* article on March 28, 1958, covering the event. We have checked the following sources: Documents of the UN Commission on Human Rights, UN Archives, *UN Journal*, *Secretariat News*, *UN Review*, as well as published books about Eleanor Roosevelt.

12. Scharffs, Figel, and Wise, *Points of Light*, 115.

Chapter 6: Attacking Root Causes and Nurturing Long-Term Solutions

1. "The Salvation Army Mission Statement," The Salvation Army, accessed February 6, 2025, https://www.salvationarmyusa.org/usn.

2. "America's Poor Are Worse Off Than Elsewhere," *Poverty Facts and Myths*, Confronting Poverty, accessed February 7, 2025, https://confronting poverty.org/poverty-facts-and-myths/americas-poor-are-worse-off-than -elsewhere.

3. "Breaking the Poverty Cycle: The Pathway of Hope," The Salvation Army, accessed February 7, 2025, https://www.salvationarmyusa.org /usn/overcome-poverty.

4. Ken Hodder, personal interview with author, September 2024.

5. Ken Hodder, personal interview with author, October 2, 2024.

6. Donna L. Hoyert, "Maternal Mortality Rates in the United States, 2021," *National Center for Health Statistics*, U.S. Centers for Disease Control and Prevention, last updated March 16, 2023, https://www .cdc.gov/nchs/data/hestat/maternal-mortality/2021/maternal-mortality -rates-2021.htm.

7. Cynthia Clark, "Church of Jesus Christ and NAACP praised for reducing infant mortality in Black communities," *Church News*, April 28, 2024, https://www.thechurchnews.com/living-faith/2024/04/28 /church-naacp-mybaby4me-memphis-hhs-recognition-washington-dc.

8. Ashley Martin, "On Juneteenth, How the NAACP and the Church of Jesus Christ Are Carrying Out a Prophet's Vision," June 19, 2023, by Church Newsroom, YouTube, https://www.youtube.com/watch?v =h850-4daNAg&t=2s.

9. "How the Church of Jesus Christ and the NAACP Are Helping Young and Expectant Mothers in Memphis," newsroom.ChurchofJesusChrist .org, November 20, 2022, https://newsroom.churchofjesuschrist.org /article/naacp-church-of-jesus-christ-memphis?filter=popular-topic.

Chapter 7: Volunteerism—The Social Movement

1. George H. W. Bush, "Remarks at the Points of Light Community Service Celebration, April 26, 1991," *Public Papers of the Presidents of the United States: George H. W. Bush* (1991, Book I, 436), April 26, 1991, https://www.govinfo.gov/content/pkg/PPP-1991-book1/html/PPP -1991-book1-doc-pg435-2.htm.

2. "Volunteering in U.S. Hits Record High; Worth $167 Billion," AmeriCorps, November 13, 2018, https://americorps.gov/newsroom/press -releases/2018/volunteering-us-hits-record-high-worth-167-billion.

3. Robert Grimm Jr., Nathan Dietz, and John Foster-Bey, "Volunteer Growth in America: A Review of Trends since 1974," Corporation for National & Community Service, December 2006, https://generosity research.nd.edu/assets/13044/volunteer_growth.pdf.

4. "Rotary International," Wikipedia, last updated January 21, 2025, https://en.wikipedia.org/wiki/Rotary_International.

5. "Rotary's two official mottoes," The Rotary Club, accessed February 7, 2025, https://www.rotary.org/en/rotary-mottoes.

6. "Rotary International's General Secretary and CEO optimistic, despite global conflict, massive migration, and natural disasters because Rotary is a peace builder," Rotary District 5040, June 21, 2023, https://www.rotary5040.org/stories/rotary-international%E2%80%99s-general-secretary-and-ceo-optimistic-despite-global-conflict-massive-migration-and-natural-disasters-beca.

7. Holly Richardson, "How do we dial down the political heat?," Opinion, *Deseret News*, July 16, 2024, https://www.deseret.com/opinion/2024/07/16/how-do-we-turn-down-political-heat-service-dignity-kindness-hope.

8. Barron Segar, personal interview with author, September 12, 2024.

9. Larry Keeley, personal interview with author, September 24, 2024.

10. Paul Cobb, "Dr. Martin Luther King, Jr. and JustServe," Morganstarmedia, January 18, 2021, https://www.youtube.com/watch?v=SHtSul2Bv9M.

11. Jason Swensen, "How the Church's JustServe initiative offers a unifying remedy for the divisive ills of the day," *Church News*, November 18, 2020, https://www.thechurchnews.com/2020/11/18/23217533/just-serve-president-ballard-unity-service.

12. Devin Thorpe, "13 Lessons From A Great Social Entrepreneur, Pamela Atkinson," *Forbes*, September 23, 2012, https://www.forbes.com/sites/devinthorpe/2012/09/23/13-lessons-from-a-great-social-entrepreneur-pamela-atkinson.

Chapter 8: It's Meant to Be Fun

1. https://www.churchofjesuschrist.org/church/news/restaurants-du-coeur-warm-meals-and-support-for-lebanons-elderly-population?lang=eng.

2. Emma Batha, "Yazidi girls sold as sex slaves create choir to find healing," *Reuters*, February 6, 2020, https://www.reuters.com/article/world/yazidi-girls-sold-as-sex-slaves-create-choir-to-find-healing-idUSKBN201039.

3. Karwan Faidhi Dri, "Music is at the heart of Yezidis' lives: Baroness Emma Nicholson," *Rudaw*, December 10, 2020, https://www.rudaw.net/english/culture/12102020.

4. Emma Nicholson, personal interview with author, April 2017.

5. Francois Pienaar, "Francois Pienaar on the impact Nelson Mandela had on the 1995 Rugby World Cup," interview by John Smit, posted October 28, 2023, Sky Sports Retro, YouTube, https://www.youtube.com/watch?v=SDMpoQuuYBY.

6. Francois Pienaar, "Francois Pienaar – BBC HARDtalk," interview by George Alayia, September 22, 2015, BBC HARDtalk, YouTube, https://www.youtube.com/watch?v=e0LaPt4lv-Y.

7. Meagan Bjorklund, personal interview with author, February 20, 2025.
8. NYT Magazine interview with Robert Putnam, July 14, 2024 https://www.nytimes.com/2024/07/13/magazine/robert-putnam-interview.html.

Chapter 9: Some Final Lessons on What Can and Cannot Be Done

1. Jimmy Carter, "Energy and the National Goals A Crisis of Confidence," *American Rhetoric Top 100 Speeches*, American Rhetoric, delivered July 15, 1979, https://www.americanrhetoric.com/speeches/jimmycartercrisisofconfidence.htm.
2. Jimmy Carter, "Farewell Address to the Nation," The American Presidency Project, delivered January 14, 1981, https://www.presidency.ucsb.edu/documents/farewell-address-the-nation-0.
3. "2011 Tōhoku earthquake and tsunami," Wikipedia, last updated February 2, 2025, https://en.wikipedia.org/wiki/2011_T%C5%8Dhoku_earthquake_and_tsunami.
4. "Traumatic Events and Post-Traumatic Stress Disorder (PTSD)," National Institute of Mental Health, last reviewed February 2025, https://www.nimh.nih.gov/health/topics/post-traumatic-stress-disorder-ptsd/index.shtml.
5. Yotam Polizer, personal interview with author, September 17, 2024.
6. Lloyd Pendelton, papers in the author's possession.

Chapter 10: The Work Is Now Yours

1. The Complete Works of Lao Tzu: Tao Teh Ching and Hau Hu Ching by Hua Ching Ni, January 1, 1995; Sevenstar Communications.